THE
STRUCTURE OF
CLASSICAL ECONOMIC THEORY

THE
STRUCTURE OF
CLASSICAL
ECONOMIC THEORY

Robert V. Eagly

New York
Oxford University Press
London 1974 Toronto

TO
Alice Hendrickson Eagly

Preface

This book is an interpretative study in the history of economic theory. It presents the analytical structure of classical economics and provides an integrative statement of the significant contributions to economic analysis from the Quesnaysian Revolution in the mid-eighteenth century to the Walrasian Synthesis in the late nineteenth century. The work is concerned with the way in which the analytical structure of classical economics served to organize inquiry and give direction to the development of economic theory for well over a century. Since the structure or gestalt of classical theory is the central focus of the study, the contributions to the analytical apparatus of classical economics that are assembled together here are defined with respect to the broader scope of classical theory. Similarly, individual economists are named in this study only with respect to their most significant contributions to the analytical structure of classical economics.

It is my hope that the book's gestalt approach will be useful both to specialists, who are interested in having an encompassing analytical framework for further research in classical economics, and to non-specialists, who are interested in having a concise and integrated survey of the development of economic theory in the period prior to the end of the nineteenth century.

I owe a debt of gratitude to a number of persons who read and commented on the manuscript of this book. In particular, I would like to give a special thanks to Royall Brandis (University of Illinois) and Jürg Niehans (Johns Hopkins University), and to express my appreciation to Leona Capeless (Oxford University Press), Warren S. Gramm (Washington State U.) and Stephen T. Worland (U. of Notre Dame). Finally, permission to use material which appeared in the *Journal of Political Economy* (parts of chapters two and six) and in the *Scottish Journal of Political Economy* (part of chapter four and the accompanying appendix) is gratefully acknowledged.

R.V.E.

Amherst, Massachusetts
August 1973

Contents

THE
STRUCTURE OF
CLASSICAL ECONOMIC THEORY

Overview of
the Analytical Structure **1**
of Classical Economic Theory

Construction of the analytical structure of classical economic theory is a particularly important task for the history of economic thought. Because the classical approach dominated economic theorizing for almost a century and a half and has formed the basis for modern economics, classical theory deservedly looms large in the history of economics. In this study, classical economics is treated with prime emphasis given to its unifying theoretical structure. This work synthesizes the principal components of classical economic theory in a way intended to elaborate the conceptual framework or gestalt of the classical system.

According to my reconstruction of classical economics, the analytical structure of classical theory is grounded fundamentally in a single major concept: *capital*. The centrality of capital within classical economics cannot be overemphasized. The capital concept is the well-spring of modern economics. It defined a new scientific frontier and posed problems of an analytical nature that absorbed the time, talent, and attention of generations of practitioners in the field. In all, the capital concept provided the analytical schema around which the component parts of classical economic theory are built.

As the first classical economist, François Quesnay promulgated the conceptual centrality of capital. Quesnay specified the supply side of his aggregate model in terms of a relationship between capital inputs on the one hand and commodity outputs on the other. In a very direct way, this set the groundwork for the basic classical model in which output was defined essentially as a function of a single reproducible factor of production, i.e., capital. Consider first of all the nature of capital as presented in the Quesnaysian Revolution and as defined by latter-day classical economists: Capital was defined to be a comprehensive collection of commodities which included everything required for production. Of the total capital stock, part was seen to enter the production process directly in its commodity form as machines or raw materials; and part was seen to be used indirectly, being first transformed via the labor market into labor power before it entered the production process. In broad outline, then, the basic classical model focused on the production of commodities by means of commodities. The division of the total capital stock was the leading problem in this basic model. The question was posed as to how the total capital stock was allocated or divided up between fixed capital (machines) and variable capital (raw materials plus wages fund). This question followed from and may be viewed as posed by the classical capital concept itself. Such propositions that output is a function of capital, that capital stock is necessarily on hand prior to production, and that capital stock is divided between fixed and variable categories were already set down by Quesnay. The question concerning *how* the total stock of capital was divided was a natural extension of this line of inquiry. In retrospect, the steps taken by classical economists in dealing in greater detail with the allocation problem formed (or unfolded) many of the main characteristics of the analytical structure of classical economic theory.

Perhaps the most salient consequence of the capital allocation problem was its formative impact on the very structure of classical theory, i.e., the mode of arranging the parts of the analysis. I believe that the best, and simplest, approach for describing the role of the capital concept in forming the structure of classical theory is to consider first the period-analytic structure of the basic classical model. The basic classical model concentrated on working out the details of the production process. Output was specified to be a function of previously accumulated capital stock. The allocation of the total capital stock between fixed and variable capital, the attendant determination of the labor wage rate, the consumption by productive labor, and the production of goods—all are activities that are inseparably grouped together because of the initial definition of capital stock. At the outset of this process the economy's total stock of commodities is in the form of capital stock; and at the end of this process the total stock of commodities takes the form of fixed capital plus (un-marketed) inventories of commodities. What we observe in this argument is that all production-related activites are identified as a sequence set and are specified to take place in one functional time period. There was, then, a period-analytic structure that was developed, or, rather, that emerged and took form. Each time period—each year, say—in classical theory was functionally divided into two activity periods: (1) the production period, which has already been described, and (2) the exchange period. The exchange period follows as a logical extension of the analysis of the production period. To begin with, it is helpful to keep in mind that when the total commodity output of each industry emerges from the productive process at the very end of the production period, the finished commodities are entirely the property of the capitalists. In order for production to take place the next year, it is necessary for the capitalists in each industry to reconstitute their capital stock. Capitalists, in other words, must move across industrial boundaries and exchange among themselves their specialized outputs in order to replenish their capital stocks. It is at this juncture that the exchange period enters the picture to serve in the first instance as vehicle for moving the analysis from production period to production period. Exchange was important, certainly, but only in regard to the contribution it made as clearing mechanism for capitalists in a multi-industry system, facilitating and enabling the reconstitution of capital stock.

The exchange period thus evolved as a step in classical analysis that was ancillary to study of the production period. It was quite appropriate, moreover, that the classical theory of exchange was worked out to solve the analytical problem of possible changes in total capital stock which would occur if capitalists were unable to sell all of their goods. Clearly, if capitalists failed to reconstitute their capital stock at the end of the exchange period, total capital stock would undergo a reduction and the smooth functioning (to say nothing of expansion) of the economy would be upset. Mill's Law and Say's Law were addressed specifically to this question. They formed a theoretical argument which assured that all commodities placed on the market were sold. J. B. Say contended that capitalists engaged primarily in market-oriented production. No one produced except to sell; and no one sold commodities except to purchase other commodities. With the economy's total output placed on the market at the outset of the exchange period, it was intuitively clear that one-half of the goods marketed could and would buy the other half. Accordingly, the fears of "gluts," periods in which capitalists accumulate unwanted inventories of unsold output, were declared unfounded. The hitchless exchange period meant that changes in total capital stock would then be limited to saving decisions made solely by the capitalists themselves. The economy would move smoothly from production period to production period and analysis could proceed with a more limited and more manageable set of variables.

The centrality of capital in the analytical structure of classical economic theory is also revealed in the exclusion of the money supply from an important role in classical theory. The transition from mercantilist theory to classical theory involved a restructuring of economic analysis in which economics moved from theory which held that "money matters" to theory which argued that "capital matters." The money supply was excluded from classical theory as a variable of any importance fundamentally by the underlying proposition that "only capital matters." Because output was dependent upon real capital stock on hand at the outset of the production period, it could not be affected by changes in the money supply. And since the quantity of goods bought and sold was set in the preceding production period, the money supply could have no meaningful impact during the exchange period. According to classical reasoning the only way the money supply could affect the economy was through changing the economy's total capital stock. Such an impact, however, was regarded as extremely remote, though some small allowance was made for the possibility of forced-saving under conditions of particularly acute inflation. An explanation of the relationship between the money supply and the general price level was provided by the quantity theory. But the repeated insistence by classical economic theorists until the end of the nineteenth century that the general level of prices was inconsequential served to re-emphasize the unimportance of money and to mark clearly that the money supply was largely banned from the arena of classical economic theorizing.

Considered in terms of the broader analytical schema of classical theory, the general equilibrium revolution is actually a natural extension of classical theory. General equilibrium analysis was a significant theoretical departure, but *initially* it was fully within the classical framework. The two-step period-analytic approach of early classical theory—the practice of dealing separately with the production period and the exchange period and searching for independent solutions to each—was recast by the Walrasian general equilibrium system. In the *Elements of Pure Economics*, the two activity periods were explicitly tied together; equilibrium was established simultaneously in both the exchange of commodities and in the allocation of factor inputs. As long as classical analysis of the commodity market was dominated by J. B. Say's interpretation, short-run relative prices were not fully explained. Walras made his well-recognized contribution to classical theory by remedying this omission. He specified demand functions for each commodity in the commodity market. There existed, Walras argued, a unique vector of prices at which the quantity of the *n* commodities demanded equaled the supply of each commodity, including money. The Walrasian approach drew a closed circle of interdependence between product and factor markets, making it clear that equilibrium in the one occurred only with equilibrium in the other. Altogether, it was an elegant system. It was, moreover, a very classical system. In it we observe the final unfolding, the final working-out, of the dominant analytical system. In retrospect, it appears that Walras's contribution constituted the last truly monumental contribution to the structure of classical economic theory.

It is indeed ironic, therefore, that the man who made and set the capstone in the structure of classical economic theory was the person whose theories struck the decisive blow against the self-same analytical structure. Walras's work completed the system of classical analysis; but working its own dialectic at the same time, it made changes in the basic classical model and posed questions that moved outside the existing analytical structure. The structural shift at the end of the nineteenth century may be characterized as a move from a theoretical schema in which capital was central to a theoretical schema in which price was central. The main battle of the end-of-the-century inter-system clash took place quietly enough. In the end, however, the capital concept, which formed the basis for the analytical structure of classical theory, was displaced. The Walrasian definition of capital originated in the analytical character of the instantaneous general equilibrium system. Specifically, Walras eliminated the variable capital component from the classical concept of capital. The goods that made up variable capital (wage goods and raw materials) were merged with the income flow of a single time period. For Walras, capital consisted narrowly of fixed capital; i.e., goods which enter production but are not used up in a single time period. Prior accumulation of the commodities which constituted variable capital was thus no longer required by economic theory. Accordingly, the responsibility formerly assigned the capitalist class dropped from sight and received no further attention beyond the Austrian school. It was, in other words, Walras's new definition of capital, not any recantation by John Stuart Mill, that killed the wages fund component of classical theory. The period-analytic approach of the basic classical model no longer served as the means for dealing with the allocation of the total capital stock. The allocation of total capital stock—its equilibrium division between fixed and variable capital components, which was a fundamental aspect of classical theory—no longer existed as a theoretical problem. Wage income, for instance, became transformed into a flow from current productive activity rather than a division of an already accumulated capital stock for current production. The close identification between labor's current productive activity and labor's wage, which was made possible by Walras's instantaneous system, was a short step removed from the marginal productivity theory. In the classical system, labor is paid a wage that is determined through the equilibrium division of an already accumulated stock; in post-Walrasian economics, the wage is an equilibrium measure of marginal (value) productivity. Labor is paid out of current, not past, output. Again we see the impact of the new definition of capital in overthrowing the structure of classical theory.

The pieces that made up the analytical structure of classical theory were constructed and put together in a logical sequence: The capital concept focused initial attention on the allocation problem. Solution of the problem, in turn, required full detailing of the production period. It was then but a short step to the puzzle-problems posed by the exchange period. All these issues were problems that arose and questions that were formulated after the initial line of inquiry into the operation of a capitalist economy was launched by the Quesnaysian Revolution. The capital concept formed the central core of classical economic theory. When capital was redefined, the structure of classical theory was overthrown. The impact of the Walrasian Synthesis was far-reaching: the classical allocation problem was eliminated from economic analysis and with it the period-analytic approach to production and exchange; capitalists, who carried the classical economy on their shoulders, were pushed into the background, and economic analysis no longer relied upon the noblesse oblige of the capitalist class; the oligarchic rule of the classical world was overthrown and replaced by the participatory democracy of the post-Walrasian world in which the preferences and utility curves of everyman were taken into consideration. In the post-Walrasian world, price—the universal stimulus to the activity of all participants in the economy—became the central focus of analysis.

The century or more that economic theory was dominated by the analytical structure of classical theory saw economics develop a formidable scientific apparatus. Theoretical advances occurred on the scientific frontier defined by the classical system. The major economic theories that appeared from 1759 to the end of the nineteenth century may be seen to fit into the classical schema. As the frontier of economic theory was pushed out, more of what was unknown was revealed. As each successive advance in analysis was made, new questions arose. Yet, in matters of scientific progress, the questions asked are at least as important as the answers. The growth of economic theory is self-sustaining as long as today's research findings raise questions that puzzle tomorrow's research economists. In the case of classical economics, it is clear that the same impetus that sustains a scientific conceptual framework can also lead to its downfall.

The Quesnaysian Revolution 2
and the Birth of Classical Theory

Considered in the broad sweep of the development of economic theory, the Quesnaysian Revolution was an impressive intellectual accomplishment. The analytical structure of Quesnay's economics effectively challenged the conventional economic wisdom of the day and (more importantly) set the orientation for scientific inquiry that was to create modern economic analysis. That classical economic theory is the child of the Quesnaysian Revolution would in itself be sufficient reason to consider the contribution of Quesnaysian economics. But in many respects Quesnaysian economics *is* classical economics—there is an aspect of unity between the two that denies any generation gap. As the first classical economist, François Quesnay conceived of and stressed the key role of capital. Therein is the common tie. In the subsequent development of economic analysis, however, the capital concept grew further in importance so that the basic classical model came to differ in some important respects from its progenitor. For instance, the Quesnaysian theory of aggregate demand, with its identification of the landlords' expenditure as the single autonomous expenditure component, was expunged from classical analysis. The differences between Quesnaysian and nineteenth-century classical theory thus became considerable. Yet despite these differences, the very heart and core of classical theory, and the essence of classical economics, is the capital concept which constitutes the rich heritage of the Quesnaysian Revolution. Quesnaysian economics cleared the way and laid the foundation for classical theory. Accordingly, it is the purpose of this chapter to examine the Quesnaysian underpinning to classical economics.

I. Aggregative Analysis in Pre-Classical Theory

Classical economic theory represents a continuance of the aggregative or macro approach to economic analysis that dominated economic thinking in the two centuries before the Quesnaysian Revolution. This section reviews mercantilist analysis (with its concern for the formulation of national economic policy and its use of aggregate variables) and constructs a mercantilist model in order to reveal the essential characteristics of economic reasoning in the period that preceded the Quesnaysian Revolution.

Early Mercantilism, 1500–1650

Throughout the mercantilist era, aggregate demand received major attention. It was construed quite simply and with little analytical sophistication: demand consisted of explicit expenditures. Mercantilist conceptualization of the static nature of the world economy—the view that trade of one country could be increased only if the trade of some other country were reduced—suggests an interpretation that world aggregate demand was fixed, or at least not amenable to control by the statesman.[1] The aggregate demand for an individual nation (D) may be specified as depending upon the size of the nation's domestically generated demand[2] ($\bar{D}$) and the trade balance (B):

(1) $D = \bar{D} + B.$

This equation, in all its simplicity, emphasizes the reasoning behind mercantilists' deep concern with the trade balance. Of the two components of aggregate demand for a given country, only the trade balance was subject to policy manipulation. The kingdom's domestic demand was beyond the control or influence of the king's magistrates, do what they might on their own account. The trade balance stood in direct contrast.

---

1. Eli Heckscher (*Mercantilism*, 2nd ed., New York, 1965, vol. 11, p. 26) writes that "It is easy to find confirmation of this mercantilist conception of the static nature of economic life." Heckscher does not, however, consider whether the "static" nature of the world economy is more appropriately conceived to be a demand or supply phenomenon. The logic of the phenomenon, nevertheless, indicates that it is a demand characteristic of the world economy. After all, the mercantilist statements that output *can*, and moreover *should*, be increased in any individual country reveal that the productive resources of the nations of the world were capable of expansion, i.e., were not static.

2. Basically, the nation's domestically generated demand ($\bar{D}$) is given. Early mercantilists did not specify the determinants of this component of aggregate demand, though it is plausible that it might be thought of as a function of population. Absence of an explanation of $\bar{D}$ points directly to the low level of abstraction in early mercantilist thought.

Exports could be increased through the granting of export subsidies; imports could be decreased by means of tariffs and import prohibitions. In all, direct controls could be imposed by the individual nation to assure that a favorable balance of trade ($B > 0$) would be achieved and maintained. A "market" solution—one in which "supply and demand" determined the trade balance for the foreign trade sector—was not envisaged. Thus, if aggregate demand was to be influenced by the statesman, it could only be affected through those policies that impinge upon the country's exports or imports. As is readily apparent, international trade between all n countries in the world is a zero-sum game. One nation's gain is another nation's loss, and the sum of balance of trade statements for all countries in the world must equal zero. National economic policy to maximize aggregate demand, output, and employment must therefore involve some struggle or antagonism between trading nations.

The aggregate supply equation in the mercantilist analysis stresses that output depends solely upon labor inputs. Three labor-related variables may be identified: the total population (P), the unemployment rate (U), and the wage rate (w). The equation would then appear:

(2) $S = \phi(P, U, w)$.

The size of population variable gained some attention from mercantilist writers, yet other than extolling the desirability of large families there was little the statesman could do to change the kingdom's population.[3] Population may be viewed here as a given, exogenously determined, magnitude. That unemployment existed in the economy was assumed as a self-evident fact by mercantilist writers. Unemployment was taken to be both explicit and disguised. To some extent, the unemployment level could be lowered, the mercantilists argued, by lowering the wage rate. The low-wage bias of mercantilism was based formally on an assumed backward-bending labor supply curve.[4] Were the wage rate reduced the supply of effort would increase as workers attempted to maintain their real income. Unemployment, thereby, would be reduced. Wage determination was seen as subject to the influence of state regulation. In the absence of supply and demand analysis, mercantilists could offer only direct action as the

---

3. Heckscher, *op. cit.*, vol. II, pp. 157–63.

4. *Ibid.*, p. 165.

  Edgar S. Furniss has called this the "doctrine of the utility of poverty" (*The Position of the Laborer in a System of Nationalism,* New York, 1965, chapter VI).

means by which the wage rate is set.[5] The wage rate may thus be regarded also as exogenously determined. In the equilibrium situation we are then left with one variable that serves to equate aggregate supply with aggregate demand, namely, the unemployment rate:

(3) $D = S$, or

(3a) $\bar{D} + B = \phi(P, U, w)$.

In equation (3a), $\bar{D}$ and P are given, B is determined by direct policy action of the statesman, and w is determined by bargaining and direct regulation. Thus, the unemployment rate (U) is the only variable left to equilibrate the system. Yet, it does not appear that the unemployment rate adjusts passively. Here, too, mercantilists regarded direct intervention—direct manipulation by the state—to be the way that adjustments in unemployment would be brought about.[6]

The mercantilist model presented here underlines the absence of *market* mechanisms in mercantilist analysis. While it is possible to discern the main variables in the mercantilist writings and even construct an explicit model in which the relationships between these variables are spelled out, it is apparent that non-market forces dominate the model and its variables at every turn. The trade balance is controlled by the customs house, the wage rate is regulated by the state or set by the capitalist, and the unemployment or idleness rate can be lowered only by the prodding of the working classes. It is not just the presence of non-market elements in mercantilist discourse, it is their *predominance* that leads to the conclusion that early mercantilists failed to develop a theory of market phenomena. That is to say, the early mercantilists did not conceptualize the market as a mechanism that was able to grind out its own equilibrium solution. It would be overly generous toward the mercantilist writers to claim that they understood the market mechanism but did not discuss it because they

---

5. Furniss, *op. cit.*, p. 157: "It is necessary that we bear in mind that the rates of wages actually paid in England at the time were supposedly determined by the Justices' assessments, and that, though the rating of wages had in large measure been allowed to die out, preceding centuries of more or less rigid wage regulation had prepared the common mind for an uncriticizing acceptance of the opinion that the income of the laboring classes must be governed by state action."

6. "For the most part," states Heckscher (*op. cit.*, p. 162), "their [the mercantilists'] solution of the unemployment problem was workhouses and poorhouses, which, on the one hand, were to provide the employment required by the people and, on the other, to maintain their diligence, the absence of which was considered the chief cause of unemployment."

recognized that certain conditions made an acceptable market equilibrium unlikely. Accordingly, they moved directly to discuss the need for non-market controls on the system. Progress in the history of economic theory should be seen in terms of improvements in the analysis of market phenomena.[7] Criticism of the market-determined equilibrium may arise. The market may not maximize those variables which some individuals consider of paramount importance. Nevertheless, from the analytical point of view, the failure of early mercantilists to spell out a market solution—their failure to recognize that a market solution exists—must be interpreted as their relatively complete innocence and lack of sophistication in economic theory.

Latter-day Mercantilism, 1650–1720

A significant advance in the analysis of aggregate demand took place in the last decades of *hoch merkantilismus*, the end of the seventeenth century and the beginning of the eighteenth century. As has been noted, aggregate demand in the early mercantilist era was defined in terms of explicit expenditure components. No attempt was made to inquire whether a given transaction had any further impact upon the market. The mercantilists of the early period failed to study the exchange process with any care. Most glaring was their neglect of the linkages between a favorable trade balance, the nation's money supply, and the level of aggregate demand. Early mercantilists tended to ignore the change in the money supply that accompanied a favorable trade balance. Changes in the money supply were regarded as merely a by-product of aggregate demand maximization[8]; and the relationship between the money supply variable and the level of aggregate demand had yet to be considered. Once aspects of the circular flow process were recognized, money's role in the economy could be appreciated. The turnover of the money supply (velocity) during the exchange period implied a rudimentary form of the multiplier process. Since a given supply of money would circulate and provide for the exchange of commodities worth several times the value of the money stock, it was but just a short step to propose that an increase in the money stock would increase the demand for goods by the same multiple.

---

7. This point of view can still be maintained even if the historical relativist position is accepted that the mercantilists failed to conceptualize the economic machine because the market had not yet developed sufficiently to effect automatic equilibrium in the system.
8. Heckscher, *op. cit.*, pp. 118ff.

Explicit incorporation of the money supply into the demand equation was accomplished at the beginning of the eighteenth century by the "paper money mercantilists." The new aggregate demand equation reads:

(4) $D = f(M^s)$.

Central attention is now focused on the money supply as the key independent variable.[9] Use of the money supply variable permits a statement of the determinants of both the domestic and the international demand for the country's output. The level of domestic expenditures is expressed as a function of the level of the money supply, while the foreign trade component of aggregate demand is introduced as changes in the money stock.[10] The increased sophistication of latter-day mercantilists over their predecessors in aggregate demand analysis is revealed in comparison of equations (1) and (4). While it is true that the rationale for the new theory of aggregate demand was quite primitive, and that a full statement of the analytical function of money was not yet provided, the new aggregate demand equation at least posed the question and made some progress along the way in answering the issue as to how money could be regarded as the key independent variable on the demand side of the model. Underlying this conceptualization of the role of the money supply was the vision of a circular flow of goods and money. Recognition of money's transactions function as medium of exchange rises above the mere commonplace when the transactions function is identified with a specific behavioral response of individual participants in the market-place. The money supply is then seen to elicit, as it were, a conditioned response on the part of persons who sell goods or services and receive a money revenue in return. Money income or revenue received by the individual is the basis for that individual's expenditures. Aggregate demand is then generated by a stream of income → expenditures → income interactions in the circular flow. By the end of the eighteenth century the functional relationship between aggregate demand and the money supply was specified. The decisive step in this direction was conceptualizing the velocity of the

9. John Law, *Money and Trade Considered*, 1705, *passim*. For example, p. 13: "Domestick trade depends on money. A greater quantity employes more people than a lesser quantity." Also *cf.* John Asgill, *Several Assertions Proved in Order To Create Another Species of Money than Gold and Silver* (1696).

10. It should be noted that paper-money mercantilists, such as John Law, broke the link between specie and the money supply. Issuance of paper money by the national bank meant that the money supply could be independent of the trade balance.

money supply and a recognition that the demand generated in the market was an interaction of the money supply and its velocity.

The analysis of aggregate demand evolved considerably in sophistication during the mercantilist era. The assignment of a key role to the money supply meant evolution from a non-abstract notion of aggregate demand that encompassed only the immediate activity of buyers in the national market-place to an abstract construct in which aggregate demand was determined by a variable whose role can be understood only when the causal inter-relationships of the theory are specified. For the early mercantilists, demand analysis involved simply setting up two categories— one for demand generated at home and a second for demand generated in the foreign-trade sector. This categorization was not a theory of demand. There was no recognition that what transpired in one market period might have implications for the subsequent operation of the economy. The failure of early mercantilists to deal analytically with the influx of specie in their discussions of the desirability of a favorable trade balance is one measure of the low level of abstraction on which these early authors operated. Latter-day mercantilists, by contrast, developed a theory of aggregate demand that provided a statement of the relevant behavioral responses in the market-place and how these were linked to the money supply variable. Such emphasis on the market-oriented responses of individuals was a significant step toward constructing a conceptual "economic machine" with which to visualize and explain economic phenomena. The response pattern of individuals was given in greater detail by the latter-day mercantilists and set down in a way to suggest belief in the predictability of socio-economic behavior.

Economic inquiry during the pre-classical period made noteworthy progress. Already by the outset of the eighteenth century, analysis of the economic system was based on a rudimentary notion that people behave in set and largely predictable ways in response to the variables that make up their market environment. The task of economic theory is a matter of pulling out the most central variables and connecting them together in a concise theoretical structure. Latter-day mercantilists took the first step in this direction. Their efforts at envisioning a certain automatic animism or response by the "economic machine" extended to their revision of aggregate supply theory. Though the basic form of the aggregate supply function underwent no change during the entire mercantilist era, the specified *response* of supply to changes in demand conditions was revised:

latter-day mercantilists began to assume that workers regard unemployment, and the attendant consumption of leisure, to be an inferior state to
employment, and the attendant consumption of commodities. The labor
supply was seen to be elastic. Thus, if aggregate demand were to increase
there would be no worry about recruiting labor in order to increase
aggregate supply. Equilibrium in the macro model of latter-day mercantilists,

(5a) $D = S,$

and by substitution from equations (2) and (4),

(5b) $f(M^s) = \phi(P, U, w),$

was considered to be assured. Decreases (increases) in the unemployment
rate, U, were seen to respond automatically to increases (decreases) in the
money supply, thereby establishing market equilibrium. As set down by
John Law, additions to the money supply were introduced into the economy by those entrepreneurs who had borrowed from the national land
bank and who were undertaking some productive, labor-using enterprise.
Law's analysis thus linked an increase in the money supply to the labor
market and provided a rationale for the argument that an increase in
aggregate demand would bring about the equilibrating increase in aggregate supply.[11] What is observed here in latter-day mercantilism is a move
toward spelling out the endogenous response operative on the supply side
of the economy.

II. The Quesnaysian Revolution: An Overview

The transition to classical economics—from approximately 1720 to 1759
—was characterized by developments in the analysis of interdependence,
or inter-connectedness, among participants in the market economy. Basic
to the construction of a circular-flow model was the explicit recognition
that one person's expenditure is another person's income. John Law had
considered a three-cornered "circular" flow, involving exchange between
landlords, farmers, and artisans.[12] But the most elaborated statement of
the circular-flow process prior to Quesnay was made by Law's contem-

---

11. Specifically, John Law (*op. cit.*, p. 90) assumes a real bills doctrine: ". . . Few if any
borrow money to keep by them."
12. *Ibid.*, pp. 97–101.

porary, Richard Cantillon. The three-cornered exchange studied by Cantillon[13] is drawn in Figure 2–1. In Cantillon's conceptualization, the

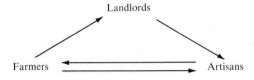

Landlords

Farmers

Artisans

FIGURE 2–1 Cantillon's Circular Flow

mainspring of the exchange process is the landlord class.[14] That is to say, Cantillon elected to take the landlords' expenditure as the point of entry into the circular-flow process. The landlords' expenditure, in effect, is specified to be the single *autonomous* expenditure in the circular flow. Designation of the autonomous variable is strictly arbitrary in the sense that the demand theory chosen determines the point at which the analysis enters into the continuous whirl of transactions that take place in the circular flow. Each expenditure generates an equal amount of income; and, in turn, expenditures are made out of income. Cantillon's own process analysis stresses this point. It is just a short step from this premise to a statement that national income is the sum total of all expenditures made in a given time period.[15] Thus, with the individual expenditures of $E_1, E_2, E_3,$ $\cdots E_n$, and the corresponding increments to national income of $Y_1, Y_2, Y_3,$ $\cdots Y_n$, the *process* of national income determination may be described as set forth in Figure 2–2. From this simple heuristic device it can be seen quite readily that the identification of the autonomous expenditure component in the system—i.e., the specification of the point of entry into the circular flow—is of crucial importance. Once E_1 is identified, the set of transactions for the exchange period is put into motion and the interdependencies between income and expenditure then generate the nation's aggregate income, $\sum_1^n Y_i$, for the period. Cantillon's analysis specifies that the first expenditure to take place in the exchange period, E_1, is the land-

13. Richard Cantillon, *Essai sur la nature du commerce en générale* (*c.* 1730), London: Frank Cass & Co., 1959, pp. 121–37.

14. Cantillon specifies that the landlord class receives rent payments from the farmers. The landlords then start the circulation of the economy's money stock by purchasing goods from the cities. *Ibid.,* pp. 123–35.

15. Provision must be made of course to exclude double-counting.

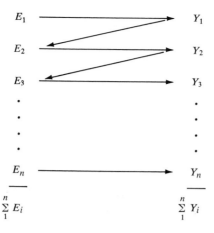

$$E_1 \longrightarrow Y_1$$

$$E_2 \longrightarrow Y_2$$

$$E_3 \longrightarrow Y_3$$

$$E_n \longrightarrow Y_n$$

$$\sum_{1}^{n} E_i \qquad \sum_{1}^{n} Y_i$$

FIGURE 2–2 Expenditure-Income Interactions

lords' expenditure of their rent income. This conceptualization of the exchange process was a major analytical advance in economic theory. What Cantillon accomplished was a creation of a quasi "real" theory of aggregate demand which, especially when later developed by Quesnay, stood as a direct alternative to the monetary aggregate demand theory offered by the latter-day mercantilists. Identification of the landlords' expenditure as the mainspring of aggregate demand pointed to the possibility of disengaging aggregate demand theory from the realm of favorable trade balances or paper-money schemes.

François Quesnay elaborated the Cantillonian approach to aggregate demand theory into a sophisticated statement. Quesnay maintained the three-cornered circular flow between (1) the Proprietary Class (land-lords), (2) the Productive Class (farmers), and (3) the Sterile Class (manu-facturers and artisans), and began the exchange process with the Pro-prietary Class's expenditure. Quesnay, however, went on to construct a model of the expenditure-income interactions that provided a determinant (and converging) series. He presented his statement of the demand equation in graphic format, specifically the zigzag diagram of the *Tableau économique*.[16] The zigzag is an explicit statement that one class's expendi-tures are a function of its income. The exchange process takes the form specified in Figure 2–3. The rent income of the Proprietary Class is entirely expended for the output of the Productive Class (food, fodder, etc.) and for the output of the Sterile Class (manufactured goods, luxury commodities, etc.). These initial expenditures in the exchange process set

---

16. François Quesnay, "The 'Third Edition' of the *Tableau Economique*," contained in *The Economics of Physiocracy* (Ronald L. Meek, editor), London: George Allen & Unwin, 1962, pp. 126–37.

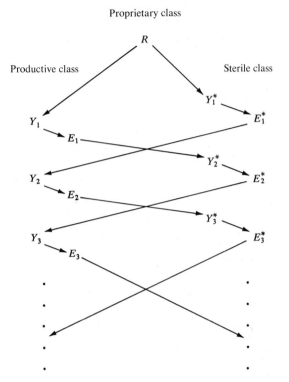

FIGURE 2–3 Zigzag Transactions of Quesnay's *Tableau économique*

in motion an infinite series of exchanges. Quesnay's analysis utilizes the geometric progression of the zigzag to indicate the infinite series and assures that the series converges by explicitly specifying the propensity to spend out of received income to be less than unity. The Proprietary Class's expenditure of its rent income, R, constitutes the autonomous expenditure component in the Quesnaysian analysis.

It is, nevertheless, on the supply side of aggregate analysis that Quesnay made his greatest contribution—and, in retrospect, the single greatest analytical contribution made in the history of economic thought. Quesnay's conceptualization of *capital* signified a complete rethinking of the aggregate supply function. Moreover, the capital concept opened an entirely new set of questions—a new line of research—that defined the dominant direction of intellectual inquiry in economics for the next century. Quesnay specified that aggregate supply was a function of the country's capital stock and he emphasized that economic growth necessarily requires an increase in capital stock. An overview of Quesnay's system can be constructed quite simply in generalized functional form. By limiting the model to one sector, aggregate demand is specified as a function of the Proprietary Class's expenditure of its rent income, R, and aggregate supply is a function of total capital stock, K. That is,

(1) $D = g(R)$,

(2) $S = \psi(K)$, and

(3) $D = S$.

In all this we observe a continuation of the *macro* character of analysis that had characterized economic inquiry since the sixteenth century. Classical theory emerged in a dominant tradition of aggregative analysis and this emphasis was to continue for over a century. Attempts to push economics into micro analysis and a concern with individual commodity markets (Cournot, Hermann, Mangoldt) had exceedingly little impact prior to the 1870's. The scope of classical analysis was aggregative in character. Study of aggregate inputs and aggregate outputs was central to classical inquiry. All in all, then, it is well to keep in mind that classical economics is essentially macro economics.

III. The Basic Quesnaysian Model

Quesnay not only set down the fundamental classical proposition that commodities are produced by means of commodities, he also specified the manner in which the inputs of commodities (i.e., total capital stock) are subdivided into functional groupings. Specifically, Quesnay divides total capital stock into two main categories: (1) fixed capital and (2) circulating capital. Both the capital concept and its two-part division dominated economic thinking for the next century and a half.

Quesnay's *Tableau économique* describes a macro economy in a condition of static equilibrium. While Quesnay did not go beyond comparative statics in analyzing the dynamic properties of his model, the functional relations that make up his theoretical structure are spelled out in sufficient detail to permit analysis of the economy's growth path over time. Construction of a Quesnaysian model of dynamic equilibrium proceeds from the analytical relationships set down by Quesnay. The supply functions of the model are based on the capital structure underpinning the *tableau*, and the demand functions are based on the zigzag transactions recorded in the *tableau*. Analysis of the properties of the dynamic Quesnaysian model not only provides a more coherent statement of the functional relations and the theoretical structure of Quesnaysian theory but also places the historical role of the theory in new perspective.

Static Equilibrium

In order to give an overview of production and exchange in the Quesnaysian world, the sequence of the economic process in the static-equilibrium version of Quesnay's model is presented in Table 2–1. Steps 2 and 3 emphasize the supply side of the model, with the annual advances (circulating capital) singled out as the key factor of production. To increase the output of agricultural or manufactured goods it is necessary first to increase the sector's capital stock. Capital accumulation is prior to and a condition for increased output capacity in either sector. In the case of both the Productive Class and the Sterile Class, circulating capital is held in the form of agricultural commodities. These take the form of raw materials and wage goods that are consumed during the production process (Step 3). Note that Table 2–1 specifies that production in both sectors takes place during the same time period. Original advances (fixed capital), which take the form of manufactured capital instruments, do not appear explicitly in the *tableau*, although replacement of depreciated original advances is recorded, as in Steps 4 and 6.

The demand side of the analysis appears in the original *tableau* as a set of zigzag lines. It gives an income-expenditure pattern that shows how expenditures are made out of income and how one sector's expenditures become another sector's income. If we know the rent income of the Proprietary Class and are given each sector's propensities to spend out of received income for (1) agricultural goods and (2) manufactured goods, we can, by and large, determine the level of demand in the economy. Step 5 of Table 2–1 notes the demand side of the model. The zigzag process (not drawn) starts in motion as the landlords make their single, once-for-all expenditure of the period. From this point on, the other two sectors spend out of received income. If the propensities (average = marginal) to spend received income for agricultural goods and manufactured goods are each assumed equal to 0.5 for all sectors, the zigzag phase of the exchange process leaves the money supply equally divided between the Productive Class and the Sterile Class. In Step 5b, the final step of the exchange process, the Sterile Class makes a single, non-reciprocated purchase of

TABLE 2–1

Sequential Analysis of the *Tableau économique*

SEQUENTIAL STEPS DURING THE PRODUCTION-EXCHANGE PERIOD	ASSET HOLDINGS OF EACH GROUP AT END OF EACH SEQUENTIAL STEP (ORIGINAL ADVANCES NOT SHOWN)		
	Productive Class	Proprietary Class	Sterile Class
1. At outset of production period the Productive Class and the Sterile Class hold their stocks of annual advances. The total money supply is held by the Productive Class.	$2A$ $2G$		$2A$
2. Rent payment to the Proprietary Class is made by the Productive Class, thus liquidating the obligation accumulated during the course of the preceding period.	$2A$	$2G$	$2A$
3. Production takes place, during which process the stocks of working capital are consumed.	$5A$	$2G$	$3M$
4. Depreciated original advances are replaced in the Sterile Class.	$5A$	$2G$	$2M$
5. Exchange between the three sectors takes place:	$2A$ $1M$	$1A$ $1M$	$2A$
a) The *zigzag phase* (the reciprocal flow of expenditures and income, initiated by the expenditure of the Proprietary Class and carried on subsequently between the Productive and the Sterile Classes);	$2G$		
b) The single purchase of agricultural goods by the Sterile Class at the end of the period. During the zigzag phase the money holdings of the Sterile Class grow to one unit of money. The one unit of agricultural goods obtained in exchange for this one unit of money is set aside for part of the annual advances for the next period.			
6. Consumption takes place in the Proprietary Class. The Productive Class uses its manufactured goods to replace its depreciated fixed capital (original advances).	$2A$ $2G$		$2A$

Note: Symbols used are: A, agricultural output; G, money; and M, manufactured goods.

agricultural goods. Quesnaysian analysis of aggregate demand in the *tableau* gave rise to several recommended policy measures: Hoarding should be discouraged and, if possible, eliminated entirely; and taxes should be levied on rent income, not commodity sales, because excise taxes would act as a "leakage" in the circular flow and would reduce aggregate demand.

At the end of the production-exchange period and after the remaining consumption takes place, the Productive Class and the Sterile Class are left holding their replenished stocks of working capital (Step 6). The scene is set, therefore, for the next production period. As long as the economy continues to reproduce its working capital and replaces depreciated fixed capital, supply in the next period will equal supply in the current period. And as long as there is no change in rent or the propensities to spend, demand in the next period will not differ from its level in this period. In short, static equilibrium prevails.

Dynamic Equilibrium

Dynamic equilibrium requires that demand increase at the same rate as supply. Quesnay's *tableau* model embodies the analytical building blocks necessary to explain changes in both demand and supply. In brief, the conditions for dynamic equilibrium can be deduced from the relationships and principles set down by Quesnay.

Presentation of the Quesnaysian dynamic-equilibrium model will use the symbols introduced in Table 2–2.

In addition, the following variables will also be used: R, the rent income of the Proprietary Class; Q_a, the quantity of agricultural commodities; and Q_m, the quantity of manufactured commodities supplied or demanded on

TABLE 2–2
List of Symbols

Variable	Productive Class Symbol	Sterile Class Symbol
Annual advances	C	C^*
Original advances	K	K^*
Depreciation rate	d	d
Gross output	A	M

the intersectoral market. Superscripts (s and d) indicate whether the variable in question is supplied or demanded. The propensities (average = marginal) to spend out of income are the Productive Class's propensity to purchase manufactured goods (a), the Proprietary Class's propensity to purchase agricultural goods (r), the Proprietary Class's propensity to purchase manufactured goods ($1-r$), and the Sterile Class's propensity to purchase agricultural goods out of income (b). Each propensity to consume out of received income is assumed to be positive and less than one. Time subscripts, $t - 1, t, t + 1$, designate production-exchange periods.

THE SUPPLY SIDE. On the supply side of the model, capital plays the key role. Quesnaysian practice states that output is a function of annual advances. This is merely a simplification of the production function and does not represent neglect of original advances, since Quesnay seems implicitly to assume a fixed ratio between original advances (fixed capital) and annual advances (circulating capital). Original advances consist of manufactured capital goods that depreciate at a rate of 10 per cent per year. Annual advances in both Productive and Sterile Classes consist of agricultural output. They are completely consumed during the productive period. In order to have annual advances on hand at the outset of the production period, the capitalists must accumulate these advances during the preceding production-exchange period.[17]

Quesnaysian writers did not work out a complete theory of capital accumulation. There is evidence, however, to support the view that the source of net additions to the economy's capital stock in the Quesnaysian model is really capitalist profit, an alternative form of economic surplus. Ronald L. Meek[18] points out that the Quesnaysians saw net additions to the economy's capital stock originating in the profit income received by capitalists who owned the economy's accumulated capital. Quesnay's followers expanded on the concept of profits as a second form of surplus in the economy. Mercier, Baudeau, and Turgot showed that both land and capital generate a disposable income.[19] Moreover, capital accumulation could be linked more directly with the profit on capital than with the net product on land. In light of these considerations, profit is defined in this

---

17. Thus, we have:

$C_t^s = C_{t-1}^d$ in the Productive Class, and

$C_t^{*s} = C_{t-1}^{*d}$ in the Sterile Class.

18. Ronald L. Meek, editor, *The Economics of Physiocracy, op. cit.*, pp. 297–312.

19. *Ibid.*, pp. 308–12.

model as the source of capital accumulation. Let π be defined as the percentage profit rate on total capital employed in the Productive Class and β as the percentage profit rate on total capital employed in the Sterile Class.[20] In the case of simple reproduction, the profit rates are zero, that is, $\pi = 0$ and $\beta = 0$. This implies that capital stock is unchaged from period to period and that static equilibrium prevails.

Not all the output of the Productive Class passes through the market. Part of total agricultural output is absorbed by the Productive Class's internal demand for annual advances to be employed in the next production-exchange period. The supply thus marketed by the Productive Class is

(1) $\quad Q_{a_t}^s = [\alpha - (1 + \pi)]C_t^s,$

where α is the ratio of total agricultural output (marketed plus non-marketed) to annual advances. Capitalists' demand for agricultural output is $(1 + \pi)C_t^s$, and $[\alpha - (1 + \pi)]C_t^s$ is the supply available to and placed on the intersectoral market.

The *Tableau* stresses that the Sterile Class is entirely dependent on the market for supplies of raw materials and food. Original advances of the Sterile Class are produced within the Sterile Class itself. Demand generated by the replacement requirements of depreciated original advances is equal to the product of the depreciation rate (d) and the stock of original advances (K_t^{*s}). The demand for net additions to original advances is generated by profits and is equal to βK_t^{*s}. The output of the Sterile Class that is supplied to the intersectoral market is then:

(2) $\quad Q_{m_t}^s = C_t^{*s}[\rho - q(d + \beta)],$

where ρ is the ratio of gross output to annual advances and q is the ratio of original advances to annual advances.

THE DEMAND SIDE. On the demand side of the model, we note that the expenditures for manufactured goods are made during the zigzag phase of the exchange process. Given rent income, R_t, received at the outset of the

---

20. Assuming that all profit is reinvested, we have:
$C_t^s = (1 + \pi)C_{t-1}^s$ and
$K_t^s = (1 + \pi)K_{t-1}^s$ in the Productive Class;
$C_t^{*s} = (1 + \beta)C_{t-1}^{*s}$ and
$K_t^{*s} = (1 + \beta)K_{t-1}^{*s}$ in the Sterile Class.

production-exchange period, the intersectoral market demand for manufactured goods is

$$(3) \quad Q^d_{m_t} = R_t \, \frac{1 - r + ar}{1 - ab} \, .$$

The expression $(1 - r + ar)/(1 - ab)$ is the *expenditure multiplier*[21] for the Sterile Class's output. For the sake of brevity of notation, this will be designated as k^*, and a time subscript will be affixed to indicate that k^* can change from period to period, depending on changes in the values for the propensities to spend out of income (a, b, and r). Intersectoral market demand for manufactured goods, $k^* R_t$, is composed of the quantity of luxury goods demanded by the landlords, $R_t(1 - r)$, and the quantity of capital goods demanded by the capitalists in the Productive Class, $R_t[ab(1 - r) + ar]/[1 - ab]$. It should be noted that the latter demand component is comprised of replacement demand for depreciated original advances plus new additions to original advances in the Productive Class, i.e., $R_t[ab(1 - r) + ar]/[1 - ab] = K^s_t(d + \beta)$. Equilibrium in the Sterile Class exists when $Q^d_{m_t} = Q^s_{m_t}$, or in terms of equations (2) and (3), equilibrium exists when

$$(4) \quad R_t \, \frac{1 - r + ar}{1 - ab} \, = C^{*s}_t[\rho - q(d + \beta)].$$

---

21. The *expenditure multiplier* for the Sterile Class (k^*) is the algebraic equivalent of the transactions recorded in the zigzag of the *Tableau*. The autonomous expenditure in the circular flow is made by the landlords who spend an amount equal to $(1 - r)R$, where R is rent and $1 - r$ is the Proprietary Class's propensity (average = marginal) to consume manufactured goods. Of this received income, $(1 - r)R$, the Sterile Class spends $b[(1 - r)R]$ for agricultural goods, of which $ab[(1 - r)R]$ flows back as the Productive Class's induced expenditure for manufactured goods. In this fashion, the landlords' expenditure of $(1 - r)R$ initiates a stream of expenditures for manufactured goods that amounts to $(1 - r)R + ab[(1 - r)R] + a^2b^2[(1 - r)R] + \cdots + a^nb^n[(1 - r)R]$ and that reduces to $R[(1 - r)/(1 - ab)]$.

A second stream of expenditures for manufactured goods is started by the Proprietary Class's purchase of agricultural goods. Of this income, amounting to rR, the Productive Class spends arR for manufactured goods in the first instance. Of this latter amount (arR), the Sterile Class returns $abrR$ to the Productive Class, which, in turn, spends a^2brR for manufactured goods. The total value of this second stream of expenditures for manufactured goods amounts to $arR + a^2brR + a^3b^2rR + \cdots + a^nb^{n-1}rR$, which reduces to $R[(ar)/(1 - ab)]$.

Adding these two streams together gives $R[(1 - r + ar)/(1 - ab)]$, where R is the autonomous expenditure variable and $(1 - r + ar)/(1 - ab)$ is the expenditure multiplier for the Sterile Class (k^*).

The expenditure multiplier for the Productive Class (k) is derived from the zigzag of the *tableau* in a similar way.

The total demand for the output of the agricultural sector is composed of three components: (1) the demand generated by the expenditures of the Proprietary Class and the Sterile Class during the zigzag phase of the exchange period; (2) the non-reciprocated expenditure made by the Sterile Class to build up its working capital to the desired level; and (3) the demand of the Productive Class itself for the amount of annual advances it desires for the next period. Of these, only the first two are expressed as intersectoral flows. The third component of demand is an internal demand expressed only within the Productive Class and does not enter the *tableau*. Let Z_t designate the demand generated by the Proprietary and Sterile Classes during the zigzag phase of exchange, and let X_t designate the single non-reciprocated expenditure made by the Sterile Class after the completion of the zigzag. The total intersectoral demand for agricultural output is then

(5) $\quad Q^d_{a_t} = Z_t + X_t.$

Of these, the first demand component may be written:

(6) $\quad Z_t = rR_t + \dfrac{R_t[b(1 - r + ar)]}{1 - ab},$

where rR_t is the demand of the Proprietary Class and $R_t[b(1 - r + ar)]/(1 - ab)$ is the demand of the Sterile Class during the zigzag phase. The next step is to determine X_t. Given the assumption that all revenue received by the Sterile Class is spent, X_t can be determined as the difference between the total revenue of the Sterile Class and the expenditures of the Sterile Class during the zigzag phase of exchange. The total sales of manufactured goods by the Sterile Class to the Proprietary and Productive Classes are equal to $R_t[1 - r + ar]/(1 - ab)$. Since the Sterile Class spends all it earns, it follows that the non-reciprocated purchase of agricultural goods by the Sterile Class is

(7) $\quad X_t = \dfrac{R_t[1 - r + ar]}{1 - ab} - \dfrac{R_t[b(1 - r + ar)]}{1 - ab} = \dfrac{R_t[(1 - b)(1 - r + ar)]}{1 - ab}.$

Substituting equations (6) and (7) into equation (5), we have the following expression for the total intersectoral demand for the output of the Productive Class:

(8) $\quad Q^d_{a_t} = \dfrac{R_t[1 + ar(1 - b)]}{1 - ab}.$

Equilibrium for the Productive Class, i.e., the agricultural sector, requires that $Q^d_{a_t} = Q^s_{a_t}$, or, in terms of equations (1) and (8),

$$(9) \quad \frac{R_t[1 + ar(1 - b)]}{1 - ab} = C^s_t[\alpha - (1 + \pi)].$$

The left-hand side of equation (9) is the total demand for agricultural output generated in the intersectoral market. For the sake of brevity, let $k = [1 + ar(1 - b)]/(1 - ab)$. This expression is the intersectoral *expenditure multiplier* for agricultural commodities. Its value can change from period to period, depending on the propensities to spend (a, b, and r). For this reason a time subscript will be added to k.

By now the key role of rent income accruing to the Proprietary Class is evident. Rent income in the Quesnaysian model is a pivotal variable. It is, in essence, the only independent variable on the demand side of the model. As equations (3) and (8) indicate, rent multiplied by the relevant expenditure multiplier determines the level of market demand in the intersectoral market. This relation is strongly suggestive of the Keynesian method of determining the level of aggregate demand as the product of autonomous investment times the Keynesian multiplier. Yet, despite the fact that rent income is the most important single variable on the demand side of the *tableau*, Quesnay did not theorize about the determinants of the level of rent income. Altogether, Quesnay had no theory of factor payments or relative income shares. The *tableau* drawn by Quesnay suggests that rent is equal to the zigzag expenditures for agricultural goods, that is, $R_{t+1} = Z_t$ (see eq. (6)). This had heuristic advantages that Quesnay exploited. As stated in equation (6), $Z_t = hR_t$, where $h = [r + b(1 - r)]/(1 - ab)$. Quesnay's assumption that $a = b = r = 0.5$ dictated that $h = 1$ and $R_{t+1} = R_t$. Static equilibrium was thus ensured. Changes in h due to changes in the propensities to spend above and below 0.5 would respectively increase and decrease rent from period to period. The change in rent would be cumulative, since $R_t = hR_{t-1}$. But this is not a theory of rent determination. It is merely a device conceived to illustrate the proposition that landlords would benefit as the demand for agricultural output was increased. As rent income increased, Quesnay argued, the *impôt unique* would constitute a smaller relative burden on the landlords. He wished to show the *direction* of change in rent income, not the level of rent income. His exposition did not go beyond that goal.

DYNAMIC EQUILIBRIUM Dynamic equilibrium requires that demand increase at the same rate as supply. For the Productive Class this condition can be described as follows:

$$(10) \quad \frac{Q^d_{a_t} - Q^d_{a_{t-1}}}{Q^d_{a_{t-1}}} = \frac{Q^s_{a_t} - Q^s_{a_{t-1}}}{Q^s_{a_{t-1}}}$$

Substituting equations (1) and (8) into equation (10), assuming that π is constant, and simplifying, we obtain a statement of dynamic equilibrium for the Productive Class:

$$(11) \quad \sigma_t = \frac{\pi + 1}{\gamma_t} - 1,$$

where σ_t is the percentage rate of change in rent, $(R_t - R_{t-1})/(R_{t-1})$, and $\gamma_t = k_t/k_{t-1}$. As indicated in equation (11), the total demand for agricultural goods is increased in response to an increase in either the rent income of the Proprietary Class or the expenditure multiplier.

Dynamic equilibrium in the Sterile Class requires that the demand for manufactured goods increase at a rate equal to the rate of increase in the output of manufactured goods:

$$(12) \quad \frac{Q^d_{m_t} - Q^d_{m_{t-1}}}{Q^d_{m_{t-1}}} = \frac{Q^s_{m_t} - Q^s_{m_{t-1}}}{Q^s_{m_{t-1}}}$$

Substituting equations (2) and (3) into equation (12), and assuming β to be constant, we obtain a statement of dynamic equilibrium in the Sterile Class:

$$(13) \quad \sigma_t = \frac{\beta + 1}{\gamma_t^*} - 1,$$

where $\gamma_t^* = k_t^*/k_{t-1}^*$.

Dynamic equilibrium for the aggregate Quesnaysian model requires a balanced expansion of both the agricultural and the manufacturing sectors. When the propensities to spend out of income are constant, γ and γ^* have unity values. Aggregate dynamic equilibrium then requires:

$$(14) \quad \sigma = \pi = \beta.$$

Equilibrium growth, therefore, implies that the rate of return to capital is the same in both sectors of the economy, that is, $\pi = \beta$. Changes in the propensities to spend out of income alter the rate of return on capital in the two sectors during the transition phase as the economy shifts to a new equilibrium growth path. Once capital is optimally allocated between the two sectors, a uniform return to capital is re-established and the economy moves along a time path described by equation (14). The impact of changes in the expenditure multipliers upon dynamic equilibrium will be discussed in the next section.

Policy Implications of Quesnaysian Analysis
Economic growth was the objective of Quesnaysian policy. To promote this objective, the Quesnaysians sought to influence both demand and supply sides of the model. First, they examined the impact of changes in the propensities to spend (a, b, and r) upon the expenditure multipliers (k and k^*). They stressed that an increase in r, the propensity of the Proprietary Class to purchase agricultural goods, would cause k to increase and k^* to decrease. This contention is fully supported by analysis of the expenditure multipliers. Likewise, it was correct to insist that an increase in the Sterile Class's propensity to purchase agricultural goods (b) would cause an increase in k. But Quesnay and his followers did not consider that an increase in b also causes an increase in k^*. The Quesnaysians thus neglected some of the interdependencies between the Productive and Sterile Classes that are built into the *tableau*. It should be noted that analysis of the expenditure multipliers in the Quesnaysian model reveals an increase in both k and k^* when a, the Productive Class's propensity to spend income for manufactured goods, increases.[22] This point was ignored by doctrinaire Quesnaysians.

When all the parameters of the model are held constant, dynamic equilibrium requires that $\sigma = \pi = \beta$. If it is assumed that σ is constant, any change in the expenditure multipliers will shift the growth paths of the Productive and Sterile Classes. Consider the impact of an increase in r that causes k to increase and k^* to decrease. The profit rate in agriculture will increase and the profit rate in manufacturing will decrease, very possibly becoming negative. Temporarily, $\sigma < \pi > \beta$. When the shift in the growth path has been completed, σ, π, and β are once again equal. In the process, capital is reallocated in the economy. Once the equilibrium ratio of rent to annual advances is established for each sector, this ratio is

---

22. Sir James Steuart's growth model focuses on the impact of changes in a upon the expenditure multipliers and the economy's growth path. Cf. Robert V. Eagly, "Sir James Steuart and the 'Aspiration Effect,' " *Economica*, N.S., XXVIII, February 1961, pp. 53–61.

stabilized. Since in dynamic equilibrium, $\sigma = \pi = \beta$, rent and annual advances increase at the same rate. The equilibrium ratio of rent to annual advances, R_e/C_e^s, specified in terms of the parameters of the model, is

(15) $\quad \dfrac{R_e}{C_e^s} = \dfrac{\alpha - (1 + \pi)}{k_t} \quad$ in the Productive Class,

and

(16) $\quad \dfrac{R_e}{C_e^{*s}} = \dfrac{\rho - q(d + \beta)}{k_t^*} \quad$ in the Sterile Class.

It is seen from equations (15) and (16) that a change in k and k^* resulting from (say) a change in r alters the ratio of rent to annual advances that is compatible with dynamic equilibrium in the model. An increase in r raises k and reduces the equilibrium (R_e/C_e^s) ratio in agriculture. The same increase in r reduces k^* and increases the equilibrium (R_e/C_e^{*s}) ratio in manufacturing. Thus, changes in the pattern of demand, by acting upon the rate of return to capital, allocate capital between agriculture and manufacturing. Given constancy in the ratio of fixed capital to working capital, an index of the equilibrium distribution of capital between the two classes can be specified as:

(17) $\quad \dfrac{C_e^{*s}}{C_e^s} = \dfrac{k_t^*[\alpha - (1 + \pi)]}{k_t[\rho - q(d + \beta)]}.$

Distribution of income in the model can be inferred, at least insofar as the rent share is concerned. Aggregate equilibrium income is equal to the sum of the products of rent and the expenditure multipliers, that is, $R(k + k^*)$. The ratio of rent to aggregate income is then $1/(k + k^*)$. Quesnaysian policy recommendations to increase r imply a decrease in the relative share of income going to the landlords.[23] This finding gives some support to the contention that there are anti-landlord overtones to Quesnay's

---

23. The change in the rent share resulting from a change in r depends on the values assigned to the other spending propensities, a and b. An increase in r will cause a decrease in the relative income share going to the landlords as long as $a < 1/(2 - b)$. The values that Quesnay assigned to these propensities (that is, $a = b = 0.5$) fall in this range.

A *ceteris paribus* change in either a or b will cause changes in $k + k^*$ in the same direction; a *ceteris paribus* change in r also causes $k + k^*$ to move in the same direction, but only as long as $a < 1/(2 - b)$. If the propensities to consume agricultural goods and manufactured goods out of received income are the same in each sector, that is, if $r = (1 - a) = b$ and $(1 - r) = a = (1 - b)$, the value of $k + k^*$ will increase as r increases, and $k + k^*$ will decrease as r decreases.

analysis. At the same time, however, it can be noted that the relative rent share decreases as the absolute level of rent and market expenditures increases.

Taxation policy was evaluated by the Quesnaysians in terms of the supply and demand impacts of different types of taxes. A tax with incidence on the annual and original advances would directly reduce the economy's productive capacity. Likewise, taxes whose incidence fell on capitalist profit would slow down capital accumulation and the expansion of the economy's productive capacity. On the demand side of the model, indirect taxes would act as expenditure leakages. The multipliers would be reduced by the introduction of a sales tax.[24] Moreover, Quesnay seems to imply that sales taxes, even with a balanced budget on the part of the government, would reduce national income, a sort of balanced-budget deflator. By contrast, a direct tax on rent income—the *impôt unique*—was the preferred form of taxation. Provided that the propensities to spend (as between agricultural and manufactured goods) were the same for the government and the landlords, the direct tax on rent income would not affect the expenditure multipliers and therefore would not change the level of expenditures generated in the economy.[25] A given total expenditure by landlords and the government would thus generate a higher national income with the *impôt unique* than with excise taxes.

---

24. With a uniform sales tax, u, imposed on the sale of all marketed goods, the expenditure multipliers become $(1 - u)[(1 - r) + ar(1 - u)]/[1 - ab(1 - u)^2]$ for the Sterile Class and $(1 - u)[1 + ar(1 - b)(1 - u)]/[1 - ab(1 - u)^2]$ for the Productive Class.

25. Aggregate demand in the basic Quesnaysian model is a function of an autonomous expenditure, A. In the absence of government in the model, the rent income spent by the landlord class, R, constitutes the autonomous expenditure. That is, $R = A$. If, in the case when government is included, tax revenue is entirely derived from taxes on land rent (the *impôt unique*) the disposable income and assumed expenditure of the Proprietary Class would be $R(1 - u)$, where u is the tax rate. Government revenue would be uR. Assuming that the government expenditures, G, equal its tax revenue, the model's autonomous expenditure would be unchanged. Since $A = R(1 - u) + G = R(1 - u) + uR = R$, it is clear that a single tax on rent would leave the aggregate demand of the economy unchanged, provided of course that the propensity of the government to spend for agricultural and non-agricultural output was the same as that of the Proprietary Class.

The Basic Classical Model 3

Classical economic theory, spanning over a century from F. Quesnay and A. Smith to K. Marx, J. S. Mill, and beyond, developed considerable unity in its internal structure. To a very great extent this unity of formal analysis was the direct consequence of the introduction of a new theoretical construct—capital. Capital provided the central schema, or analytical structure, that gave a sweeping overview of economic processes and provided a mode of analysis that served as the main vehicle for progress in economic theory from 1759 to the end of the nineteenth century. Clearly, the centrality of capital in classical analysis is aptly revealed in the title Karl Marx selected for his *magnum opus*. Following Quesnay's lead, classical economists defined capital quite comprehensively to include command of all the reproducible inputs used in production, i.e., machinery, raw materials, and labor. The degree of abstraction in the capital concept was considerable. To consider the initial allocation process, the total capital stock was conceptualized to consist not of use-specific commodities but of abstract commodities "in general," a malleable, putty-like commodity unit that could be allocated either to the wages fund or to the stock of machinery. Such an abstraction permitted classical analysis to concentrate on the problem of capital allocation.

The basic classical problem of capital allocation may be depicted in terms of a simple process diagram: As indicated in Figure 3–1, the production period starts (on the left) with a given stock of capital and is completed (on the right) with the output of commodities. Quite simply, output is a function of capital stock. The intervening analytical steps, however, embrace the capital allocation problem that constituted the central focus of classical economics. The allocation process requires that machinery and labor be brought together in the ratio dictated by existing technology. What this means is that part of the total capital stock will be used directly in commodity form (i.e., as machines and raw materials) and part of the total capital stock will be used indirectly (i.e., as commodities "transformed" into labor power). In order to subdivide total capital stock into (1) fixed capital (machinery) and (2) circulating capital (wages fund), the analysis must at the same time determine the ratio at which commodities are transformed into labor—i.e., the wage rate. Once the total capital stock has been fully allocated and equilibrium prevails, the capitalists have on hand machinery and labor in the technologically correct proportions. Then, with the allocation process completed, production takes place, commodity output is brought forth, and the production period comes to a close. In all this, the factor market is a general equilibrium mechanism that optimally allocates the economy's total capital stock.

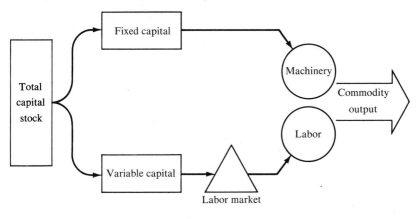

FIGURE 3–1

In this chapter, section I presents a model of the classical capital allocation process. Section II discusses the operation of the model and demonstrates that total capital stock will be fully utilized. Section III argues that the basic classical model dictated a period analysis that identified a separate production period and exchange period. Section IV constructs a disaggregated version of the basic allocative model. Section V sets forth the classical theory of relative price determination. And finally, section VI discusses the determinants of capital accumulation in classical analysis, and section VII discusses population growth.

I. The Basic Model

Capital stock in the classical economic model is divided into two major components: (1) the means of subsistence for the labor force, i.e., the wages fund; and (2) the instruments or tools of production, i.e., machinery.[1] The exact equilibrium division of the total capital stock between these two uses is determined by technological considerations and by relative market prices for labor and capital goods. Given a fixed labor-machinery ratio, additions to the total capital stock necessarily imply an increased demand for both machinery and labor. Since labor cannot be employed without being supplied the tools of production, the rational capitalist-entrepreneur in the classical model would adjust his demand for labor and machinery so that he was supplied with the technologically correct input mix. The capitalist-entrepreneur would, at the same time, demand an additional laborer and an additional machine. That labor and machinery are *jointly* demanded is a major theme underlying the classical discussion of the structure of total capital stock. It is the purpose of this section to illustrate how the classical demand for labor can be derived as a joint-demand function and to show how supply-demand equilibrium is established in the factor markets.

Classical economists, J. S. Mill in particular, implicitly assumed an exogenously fixed ratio of labor to machinery,[2] and regarded the ratio as a short-run technological parameter of the system. Let us designate this ratio as $\alpha = N/k$, where N is the number of laborers employed, and k is an index of the number of machines. This implies that the quantities of labor and machinery are jointly demanded in the following way:

---

1. A third subdivision, raw materials, is not considered in section I but is introduced in section IV of this chapter. Omission of raw materials in this introductory discussion of the basic model is in line with the typical classical treatment of the allocation problem. In practice, the combination of wage goods and raw materials was especially awkward for the main thrust of classical analysis. But rather than redefine the original Quesnaysian division of total capital stock, classical economists skirted the issue in a loose and *ad hoc* manner. Karl Marx tidied up matters by rearranging the categories. Specifically, Marx moved the raw materials component from the circulating capital category to the fixed ("constant") capital category and renamed the fund of wage goods "variable capital." In analytical terms this rearrangement is significant primarily because it permitted Marx's analysis to study the labor market with greater clarity. The importance of Marx's redefinition of the fixed and circulating components of total capital stock cannot be exaggerated.

2. The labor-machine ratio is a parameter (i.e., a variable constant) that is subject to change from forces outside the model.

(1) $N^d = \alpha k^d$,

where the superscript d indicates demand. The supply curve for machine goods, k^s, may be specified as follows:

(2) $k^s = f(p)$,

where p is the money price of machinery deflated by the money price of wage goods, and the superscript s indicates supply. It is assumed that the monetary determinants of product prices exercise the same proportional influence on the price of machinery and wage goods so that p is unaffected by changes in the money supply. Relative prices, therefore, are influenced only by technologically determined costs of production. The slope of the long-run supply curve for machinery depends upon the assumption made concerning the trend value of the returns to scale in the machine-goods industry relative to that in the wage-goods industry. Because wage goods are weighted heavily in favor of agricultural goods, diminishing returns in agriculture would dictate a decline in the price of non-wage goods in terms of wage goods. Such a situation is assumed here. Accordingly, the relative supply price for machines declines in the long run,[3] that is, $f'(p) < 0$.

A value for k^d, the demand for machinery, can be selected arbitrarily and equilibrium assumed to exist in the machine-goods market:

(3) $k^d = k^s$.

For any arbitrarily selected equilibrium in the machine-goods market, we wish to know whether the labor market is in concurrent equilibrium and, if not, what mechanism tends to push the two markets toward simultaneous equilibrium. Essentially, this is a problem in the optimum market allocation of a given total capital stock.

The given total capital stock of the economy $(\overline{K})$ is measured here in money terms deflated by the price of wage goods. It is necessarily divided between the amount allocated for wage goods and the amount allocated for machinery. Thus:

---

3. Cf. John Stuart Mill, *Principles of Political Economy* (1848; Ashley ed. 1909), New York: Augustus M. Kelley, 1969, p. 703: "The tendency, then, being to a perpetual increase of the productive power of labour in manufactures, while in agriculture and mining there is a conflict between two tendencies, the one towards an increase of productive power, the other towards a diminution of it, the cost of production being lessened by every improvement in the processes, and augmented by every addition to the population: it follows that the exchange values of manufactured articles, compared with the products of agriculture and of mines have, as population and industry advance, a certain and decided tendency to fall."

(4) $\bar{K} = wN^d + \bar{p}k^d,$

where w is the real wage rate, and $\bar{p}$ is the equilibrium price of machinery—both deflated by the price of wage goods. All the necessary relationships to derive the labor demand curve are now present. Given equations (1) and (4), along with arbitrarily selected equilibrium values for k, it is possible to locate all loci of the labor demand curve, that is, all (N_i^d, w_i). Rearrangement of the terms of equation (4) gives an expression for labor demand as a function of w:

(5) $N^d = \bar{K}/(w + \bar{p}/\alpha).$

It is apparent from equation (5) that capital accumulation increases the demand for labor.

Next, the long-run labor supply curve can be specified as:

(6) $N^s = n(w).$

As has been stated, the wage rate considered here is calculated in real terms, i.e., the money wage rate deflated by the price of wage goods. The long-run labor supply may be specified to be a function of an upward-trending subsistence wage.[4] Population is assumed to increase in response

---

4. The slope of the long-run labor supply schedule may be specified either with an optimistic or a pessimistic outlook toward the future of the working class. The optimistic approach assigns a positive slope to the long-run labor supply schedule on the premise that the subsistence level of existence tends to rise in an expanding economy as workers accustom themselves to market wages above what was previously defined as subsistence. In this connection John R. McCulloch (*The Rate of Wages* (1854), New York: Augustus M. Kelley, 1967, p. 34) writes: "The natural or necessary rate of wages is not, therefore, fixed and unvarying.... When wages rise, a period of eighteen or twenty years must elapse before the stimulus which the rise gives to the principle of population can be felt in the market. And during all this period, the labourers have a greater command over necessaries and conveniences. Their habits are in consequence improved. And as they learn to form more elevated notions of what is required for their comfortable and decent support, the natural or necessary rate of wages is gradually augmented."

John Stuart Mills tends to be pessimistic about the possibility of a positively sloped labor supply schedule, observing that "it is a much more difficult thing to raise, than to lower, the scale of living...." An increase in the standard of living, Mill indicated, required a sudden and substantial increase in wages such as that associated with the French Revolution (Mill, *op. cit.*, p. 348). Mill writes: "When, indeed, the improvement is of this signal character, and a generation grows up which has always been used to an improved scale of comfort, the habits of this new generation in respect to population become formed upon a higher minimum, and the improvement of their condition becomes permanent" (*ibid.*, p. 349).

It should be noted that the model constructed here can readily accommodate either the optimistic or the pessimistic approach without altering the analytics of the system. As presented in the text the long-run labor supply schedule features a long-run rising subsistence wage.

to short-run wage rate increases. There is a unique equilibrium population size (and labor supply) for a given amount of total capital stock. Long-run equilibrium is then determined when

(7) $\quad N^s = N^d.$

Since all points on the labor demand schedule are associated with equilibrium conditions in the machine-goods market, equilibrium in the labor market necessarily implies general equilibrium.

To summarize the argument, the system of equations is represented graphically in Figure 3–2. The α line in the NE quadrant gives the labor-machinery ratio. First, select an arbitrary value for k. We assume equilibrium in the machine-goods market and read the price of machinery from the supply curve drawn in the NW quadrant. The Z lines in the SW quadrant are drawn for a given total capital stock $(\overline{K})$ and arbitrarily selected pairs of (k_i, N_i) such that $N_i = \alpha k_i$, where $i = 1,2,3,\cdots,n$. The intercepts of the Z lines are $(\overline{K}/k_i)$ and $(\overline{K}/N_i)$. The dotted $\overline{K}$ line that appears in the NW quadrant is drawn for construction purposes to locate the Z line intercepts on the p axis. The $\overline{K}$ line is drawn for a constant quantity of total capital and is measured by the rectangle under the $\overline{K}$ line. Once the the value for k_i is selected, it is possible to see graphically the associated division of total capital between machine goods (the area of the rectangle under the machine-goods supply curve $[= k_i\bar{p}]$) and wage goods (the area of the rectangle wedged between the $\overline{K}$ line and the machine-goods supply curve $[= k_i\{\overline{K}/k_i - \bar{p}\}]$).

For purposes of illustration, select the pair (k_1, N_1). This step gives a point on the $\overline{K}$ line, which, in turn, locates the intercept of the Z_1 line in the SW quadrant. Note that each Z line is drawn from the p axis with the same slope $(1/\alpha)$. Once the Z_1 line is located, it is possible (by reading the equilibrium price of machinery, $\bar{p}$, from the machine-goods supply curve) to determine the labor wage rate, w. We now have determined the locus of the pair (w_1, N_1^d). In other words, we have located one point, X_1, on the labor demand curve. Points X_2 and X_3 are located in a similar way. The labor demand curve, N^d, in the SE quadrant is seen to intersect the labor supply curve, N^s, when $N = N_2$. Note that capital accumulation dictates a shift in the entire set of Z lines in the SW quadrant downward and to the left. This would, in turn, shift the demand for labor curve in the SE quadrant downward and to the right.

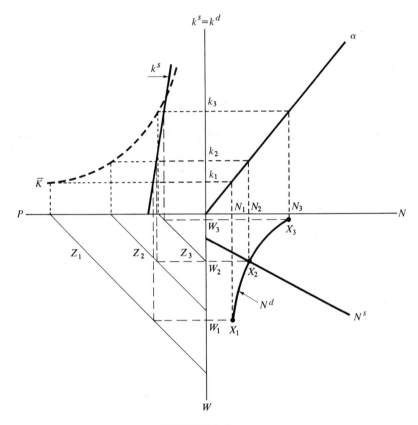

FIGURE 3–2

II. Full Utilization of Capital Stock

In the basic classical model presented above, the given amount of capital stock in the hands of the capitalists is assumed to be completely expended and fully utilized. Though this assumption assures the determinancy of the system, it is subject to challenge and is a point that did not go unnoticed by classical economists. Basically, the question posed here is whether the system behaves in such a way to prevent capitalists from keeping part of the given capital stock idle and removed from productive employment. In other words, does the system include some mechanism by which full utilization of the total capital stock is assured? This question received only scattered attention from classical economists—the issue was generally resolved by assertion of full utilization of capital by capitalists—but an answer to the question can be inferred from the logic of the classical system.

To elaborate the equilibrating mechanism that assures full utilization of total capital stock, it is useful to distinguish between two categories of excess demand for labor in the classical system described here. For want of better terms, they may be called (1) "technological excess demand" and (2) "resource excess demand." In terms of the model presented above in section I, technological excess demand for labor is defined as $0 < (N^d - \bar{N}^s) = (\alpha \bar{k}^s - \bar{N}^s)$, where $\bar{k}^s$ is the existing stock of machinery and $\bar{N}^s$ is the existing supply of labor. In the classical system, it is the labor supply, not the quantity of machinery, that is fixed in the short run. At the outset of the analysis total capital stock is comprised of generalized resources—a putty-like commodity that initially can be allocated readily either to wage goods or machine goods. When these resources are committed in fixed form as machinery, the use-specific nature of the capital resource is defined. An increment to fixed capital "hardens" the capital resource into a durable shape. Some small increment to machinery is all that need be posited to account for, and guarantee, the full utilization of the economy's total capital stock: when capital accumulates, starting from an initial general equilibrium situation, capitalists add Δk^s to their holdings of machine goods and thereby create a technological excess demand for labor $(= \Delta k^s \alpha)$. Capitalists then have an excess supply of machinery that they strive to put into operation. This condition $(0 < \Delta k^s \simeq 0$, and hence $0 < \Delta k^s \alpha \simeq 0)$ provides the basis for active competition among capitalists for available workers that continues as long as resource excess demand exists. Resource excess demand for labor is defined as $0 < (N^d - \bar{N}^s) = [\bar{K}/(w + \bar{p}/\alpha)] - \bar{N}^s$. It originates in the unexpended portion of the wages fund. When capital stock increases, starting from a condition of general equilibrium, the short-run wage rate rises to re-establish equilibrium and eliminate the resource excess demand. Rearranging the terms of this equation, we have the equilibrium wage, that is, $w = (\bar{K}/\bar{N}^s) - p/\alpha$. Recalling that Δk^s has been assumed to be very small, we conclude that the change in wage (Δw) is less than but approximately equal to $\Delta K/\bar{N}^s$.[5] The short-run equilibrium thus established represents a resource equilibrium in the sense that the resources available to demand labor (the wages fund)

---

5. Differentiation of the expression $w = (\bar{K} - \bar{p}k^s)/\bar{N}^s$ yields $dw = (dK - \bar{p}dk^s)/\bar{N}^s$. Since $dk \simeq 0$. the expression for a change in wage becomes $dw \simeq dK/\bar{N}^s$, or, in difference notation, $\Delta w \approx \Delta K/\bar{N}^s$.

are fully expended on the given supply of labor. There continues to exist, nevertheless, technological excess demand for labor, but the resource base for bidding wages up is exhausted. It is the technological excess supply (demand) of machinery, acting through the resulting techno-logical excess demand (supply) for labor, that is the dynamic element. Without it, the classical system would have no mechanism to ensure the full allocation of total capital stock and the movement from one to another general equilibrium situation in which all excess demands in all factor markets are zero, and total capital stock is fully employed.

One issue remains, however. Existence of a technological excess supply of machine goods denotes that a portion of total capital stock is unutilized in the production process. Because the capitalists receive no return from this part of their capital, they will, *ceteris paribus*, move to eliminate it entirely from their holdings. But because of the durable character of machinery, capitalists cannot free any part of their total capital stock that is already allocated to machinery without first waiting for depreciation to occur. Once the stock of machinery is depreciated by an amount equal to the technological excess supply, the resources thus freed would be dis-invested and the total capital stock would be reduced.

There is, nevertheless, a counteracting force that prevents a prompt reduction in the total capital stock from occurring: Classical theory defined the long-run propensity to accumulate as a function of the difference between the actual and the minimum acceptable profit rates. Accordingly, the propensity to accumulate by all capitalists would not be immediately stopped by the existence of unused fixed capital in the hands of a few capitalists. Capital would continue to accumulate until the increase in wages had pushed the actual profit rate down to the minimum acceptable level. Each period's net addition to total capital stock would maintain the technological excess supply of machinery and provide the additional resources to bid up wages. The economy with a stable popula-tion and a given technology would thus be propelled to a stationary state in which net investment fell to zero and wages ceased to rise. Because of a fixed technology, economic expansion in the classical model requires that population grow in response to the accumulation of capital. There must be an increase in both machinery and labor for an increase in output to take place. The classical population equation met this requirement by specifying population growth to be a function of the difference between the market and the subsistence wage rates. With the introduction of the population equation, the system becomes dynamic and questions of economic growth rise as an issue distinct and conceptually separate from the fundamental issue of the allocation of capital.

Consider the argument in terms of Figure 3–3 (which constitutes the SE quadrant of Figure 3–2). The labor market is in long-run, and short-run, equilibrium at subsistence wage w_1 and employment level N_1. The long-run labor supply schedule (N_{LR}^s) is drawn as a positive function of the real wage while the short-run labor supply schedule (N_{SR}^s) appears as a vertical line. The increment to total capital stock shifts the labor demand schedule upward and to the right from N_1^d to N_2^d. Initially, the wage rises to w_0, but, as population increases in response to this higher-than-subsistence wage, the wage rate moves downward along N_2^d. Since the labor demand schedule (N_2^d) is inelastic, the drop in wage reduces the wage bill and frees resources that are simultaneously absorbed by the purchase of machinery. When long-run equilibrium and short-run equilibrium are again simultaneously established at the higher subsistence wage level (w_2) and higher level of employment (N_2), equilibrium also prevails in the machine-goods market. The model thus permits analysis of both long-run and short-run equilibria.

III. Period Analysis in Classical Theory

Because capital constituted the single category of inputs into the productive process, the basic classical model was necessarily constructed in a period-analytic format. Two separate functional activities were en-

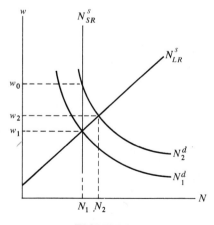

FIGURE 3–3

visioned: (1) production and (2) exchange. Each of the two sets of activites involved its own equilibrium solution. Though the production and exchange periods were seen to be interrelated, it was not until the last third of the nineteenth century that classical economics generated an integrative theory that indicated the interdependence of production and exchange activities in a general equilibrium solution.

Period analysis in the basic classical model is a heuristic device that was largely dictated by the capital concept itself. First, production required the prior accumulation of capital: the economy's capital stock had to be on hand before commodity output could be fabricated. Members of the work force subsisted on the resources that were in the hands of the capitalists at the outset of the production period. By like token, the commodity output of the current time period is destined for consumption at some later date. In the classical production period, then, the capitalist class owns the economy's total capital stock at the outset of production and owns the economy's total output when production is completed. When production activity is over, the exchange period then begins. Formally, the exchange period entails an exchange of commodities (and only commodities) among capitalists. Essentially, the capitalist class owns the total commodity output at the outset of the exchange period; and, at the end of the exchange period, the capitalist class still owns the total commodity output.[6] What takes place during the exchange period is a *distribution* of the economy's total output of commodities: Capitalists sell their own specialized output and purchase the outputs of other industries. In the process, preparation is made for the next time period. Part of total output is channeled to reconstitute the capital consumed in production; another portion of total commodity output goes to augment the total capital stock; and yet another portion is directed to either "luxury" consumption or the consumption of non-productive labor.

Classical period analysis may be depicted in terms of Figure 3–4. As has been pointed out, the allocation of the total capital stock between fixed

---

6. John S. Mill, *op. cit.,* pp. 417–18: "The capitalist, then, may be assumed to make all the advances, and receive all the produce. His profit consists of the excess of the produce above the advances." Karl Marx (*Capital* (1867), Moscow: Foreign Languages Publishing House, 1961, vol. I, pp. 184–85) takes the same view: "The labour-process, turned into the process by which the capitalist consumes labour-power, exhibits two characteristic phenomena. First, the labourer works under the control of the capitalist to whom his labour belongs.... Secondly, the product is the property of the capitalist and not that of the labourer, its immediate producer."

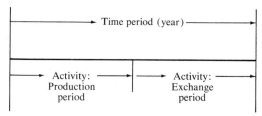

Schema of period analysis in classical theory

FIGURE 3–4

capital and circulating capital is the fundamental focus of classical analysis of the production period. Whereas the first set of commodities (machines) is employed in production directly in its commodity state, the second set of commodities is employed in production only after it has been literally "transformed" into labor power. Specifically, this latter group of commodities must be exchanged for labor power, a step at the outset of the production period that entails the determination of the labor wage rate. Once the wage rate is determined, and total capital stock fully allocated, production takes place. Total commodity output, then, is brought to the market and buying and selling takes place in the exchange period.

IV. Disaggregation of the Basic Classical Model

The basic classical model which was presented in section I of this chapter can be viewed to advantage in terms of a disaggregated model. Disaggregation emphasizes the multi-commodity nature of capital, suggests the complexity of the allocation process, and indicates the conceptual difficulty in defining the unit of measure for capital, wages, or "value" in general. This approach permits an overview of the basic classical system that suggests inter-connections between parts of classical analysis that might otherwise seem isolated or even unrelated to one another.

The Exchange Period
At the end of the production period, the output of commodities emerges from the production pipeline. Capitalists in each of the n industries $(i = 1 \cdots n)$ place their output (Q_i^s) on the market. Functionally, the exchange period serves as the time during which the capitalists reconstitute their capital stock, first by selling their outputs and then by buying commodities to replace their just-consumed stocks of circulating capital

(raw materials and wage goods) and depreciated fixed capital (machinery) as well as to make net additions to all categories of capital stock. Clearing of the market is assured by Say's Law, the "solution" for the exchange process that was adopted by classical economists. According to the classical analysis of the exchange period, production is essentially market-oriented. No capitalist produces except to place his output on the market. The supply of commodities placed on the market in this way, generates a sales revenue (R) received by the capitalists:

(1) $\quad R = \sum_{1}^{n} p_i Q_i^s,$

where Q_i^s is the given output of the ith commodity placed on the market, and p_i is the price of the ith commodity in terms of the nth commodity which is selected as the numéraire. The revenue thus received by the capitalists is immediately spent in order to permit the capitalists to purchase other commodities. The revenue spent in this way generates a demand for commodities:

(2) $\quad R = \sum_{1}^{n} p_i Q_i^d.$

And, finally, in equilibrium, the demand for commodities is equated with the supply for commodities:

(3) $\quad \sum_{1}^{n} p_i Q_i^d = \sum_{1}^{n} p_i Q_i^s.$

All in all, the total output of the economy is placed on the market and exchanged among capitalists in order to permit them to reconstitute and augment their capital stock in preparation for the next production period. In the process of exchange, relative prices are determined.

The Production Period

At the outset of the production period, a general equilibrium is established in which the joint demand for machinery, raw materials, and wage goods (transformable into labor power) fully employs the total capital stock. Given the level of technology, it is possible to specify a production co-efficient matrix for both machinery and raw materials. Coefficients in each matrix define the quantity of the jth capital resource $(j = 1 \cdots m)$ required to produce one unit of the ith commodity output $(i = 1 \cdots n)$, where $n > m$.

When combined, these two matrices yield a matrix of production co-efficients for "commodity capital"—resources that are used in production in their commodity form (i.e., machinery and raw materials). With a_{ij} representing the commodity-capital production coefficients in the matrix, the total demand for commodity capital may be written:

(4) $\quad k_j^c = \sum_{i=1}^{n} Q_i^* \, a_{ij}$,

where Q_i^* is the planned commodity output in the ith industry. The planned commodity output in each industry may be considered to be some function of last period's relative commodity prices and the current period's wage rate. What remains next to be determined is the demand for wage-goods capital.

The labor market is essentially a mechanism that transforms commodities (wage goods) into labor power. The wage which equilibrates the demand for and the supply of labor is the measure of the ratio at which wage goods are transformed into labor power. The question of the commodity composition of the laborers' "market basket" presents some conceptual difficulty. For instance, if the composition of the market basket is altered with some components increasing and other decreasing, it becomes problematic whether the wage rate has risen, fallen, or remained stable. For the sake of simplicity, let us assume a market basket that has a constant composition. That is to say, a set of commodities all of which bear constant proportion to one another. Let b_j be the set of commodities in the subsistence basic market basket. The commodity wage rate per laborer may be defined as a certain scalar multiple (λ) of the basic market basket unit (b_j). That is

(5) $\quad w = \lambda b_j$.

If the basic market basket is specified to constitute the classical subsistence wage per laborer, then when $\lambda = 1$, the wage is at subsistence, the labor supply is unchanging over time, and the system tends toward long-run equilibrium. When λ has some non-unitary value, however, the market wage diverges from subsistence and the labor supply will either increase or decrease depending on whether it is respectively greater or less than unity.

To complete the computation of the demand for wage-goods capital, let γ_i be the technologically determined set of labor-output coefficients in each of the n industries ($= N_i/Q_i$). The demand for wage-good capital is then equal to

(6) $\quad k_j^w = \lambda b_j \sum_{i=1}^{n} \gamma_i Q_i^*.$

General equilibrium prevails in the production period when the given supply of commodities that makes up the total capital stock (k_j^s) is equated with the total joint demand for machinery, raw materials, and wage goods. That is,

(7a) $\quad k_j^s = k_j^c + k_j^w,$ or

(7b) $\quad k_j^s = \sum_{1}^{n} Q_i^* a_{ij} + \lambda b_j \sum_{1}^{n} \gamma_i Q_i^*.$

Short-run equilibrium exists in the production period when the given short-run supply of labor ($\bar{N}^s$) is equated to the period's technological demand for labor ($\sum_{1}^{n} \gamma_i Q_i^*$) at an equilibrium wage rate established by means of adjustments in λ. The case of long-run equilibrium, characterized by an absence of demographically-induced changes in the short-run labor supply, prevails when the wage rate rests at the subsistence level, that is, to a level associated with $\lambda = 1$.

System Equilibrium

Profit maximization in the allocation of total capital stock requires that capital be divided in a way that equates the rate of return in all industries. System equilibrium prevails when a uniform profit rate exists throughout the economy and there is no tendency to change the division of total capital stock between industries. Any change in the economy that has a differential impact on the profitability of capital in the different industries will disturb system equilibrium. Such moves as a demand-induced change in the pattern of market prices or a technology-induced change in productivity rates would raise the profit rate in some industries or lower it in others. A reallocation of total capital stock would then take place to equalize profit rates once again. Because the pattern of relative prices established in one exchange period influences the allocation of capital stock as well as the composition of output in the subsequent production period, there is a continuous interaction between exchange and production periods. Disruption of system equilibrium, therefore, would involve a series of adjustments over several time periods in order to restore equilibrium. The relationships between profit, prices, and the allocation of capital stock over industries is explored in section V of this chapter.

V. Relative Prices and the Uniform Profit Principle

Prior to the advent of utility analysis and general equilibrium analysis, classical economics relied upon the uniform profit principle to serve as the criterion condition for identifying the optimum set of relative prices. Though relative prices in the basic classical model are determined by "supply and demand" during the exchange period, their equilibrium level is dictated by inter-industry uniformity in the profit rate. The criterion developed for indicating equilibrium relative prices, namely, the uniform profit principle, was derivative of the pattern of capital allocation in the economy at large. According to the uniform profit principle, relative prices are optimal if the rate of return to capital is at the same level in all sectors and in all industries of the economy. The uniform profit criterion thus makes relative prices dependent upon the size, productivity, and distribution of the economy's total capital stock—evidence once again of the all-pervasive importance of capital in classical theory. The seminal contributions to this theoretical task were made by David Ricardo and Karl Marx. It is the purpose here to sketch the Ricardo-Marx schema of relative price determination.

Ricardian Prices
David Ricardo's two-sector model is the pioneer effort in using the uniform profit principle as the analytical vehicle for determining relative prices. His model[7] identifies agriculture as the lead sector of the economy whose own internal profit rate sets the rate of return to capital for the whole economy. Output of the agricultural sector (Q_a) is specified to be a function of a fixed quantity of land and a variable quantity of composite factor (C_a), composed of machinery and labor in the technologically correct proportion. That is, $Q_a = f_a(C_a)$, where the fixed input is implicit in the function. For simplicity, the technological composition of the composite factor is assumed to be the same in both the agricultural and manufacturing sectors. The economy's given total capital stock is thus pre-packaged in a quantity of composite units (C), which is divided between the amount allocated to the agricultural sector (C_a) and that

---

7. For a brief exposition of Ricardo's model of relative income shares see footnote 29.

allocated to the manufacturing sector (C_m) as aggregated over all n individual industries, that is, $C_m = \sum_1^n C_i$. Expressed in grain units, the profit in agriculture per unit of composite factor (π_a) is the difference between the marginal product of the composite factor, $f'_a(C_a)$, and the consumption of composite factor, $\bar{x}$ ($=$ wage to labor plus depreciation of machinery per unit of composite factor), also expressed in grain units:

(1) $\quad \pi_a = f'_a(C_a) - \bar{x},$

where the subscript a denotes the agricultural sector. Because the agricultural production function, $f_a(C_a)$, is subject to diminishing returns due to an increasing relative scarcity of land as capital accumulates, the marginal product of the composite factor decreases as agriculture expands, that is, $f''_a(C_a) < 0$. In the closed economy, the level of agricultural output is set equal to the subsistence requirements of the community at large which are determined by the size of the population, the historically determined standard of well-being, and, at bottom, the size of the economy's capital stock.[8] Once the demand for and supply of agricultural output are equated, the quantity of composite factor devoted to agriculture is determined. The profit rate for this sector is then immediately determined.

The situation is somewhat different for the manufacturing sector, where the production function for each industry, $f_i(C_i)$, exhibits constant returns to scale and the marginal product is constant, that is, $f''_i(C_i) = 0$. The profit rate in manufacturing[9] is then

---

8. Population in the classical system can be subdivided into three groupings: first, those people linked to the productive work force whose members are employed by capital; second, those people linked to the unproductive work force whose members are employed out of the economy's net product which is a function of the economy's total capital stock; and third, those people in the upper classes—the capitalists and landlords—whose incomes depend upon the magnitude of the net product, which, in turn, is a function of capital stock. Since, in addition to tastes, expenditures for agricultural goods by each group depend upon its income, which is in turn a function of the economy's capital stock, it is possible to formulate the demand for agricultural output as a complex function of the economy's total capital stock. At bottom, of course, capital stock is the key variable of the entire classical system.

9. Equation (2) can also be written to take risk and uncertainty into account. The equation would then stand $\pi_i = p_i f'_i(C_i) - \bar{x} - \bar{r}_i$, where $\bar{r}_i$ is the given rate differential for risk and uncertainty in the ith industry relative to the general level that prevails in the agricultural sector. (Cf. David Ricardo, *The Principles of Political Economy and Taxation* (1817), London: J. M. Dent & Sons, Ltd., 1955, pp. 49–50.) Inclusion of $\bar{r}_i$ means that the uniform profit criterion, $\pi_i = \pi_a$, does not necessarily imply that market price is equal to natural price unless perceived risk is assessed at a value equal to actual resource cost. The natural price might then be redefined to include $\bar{r}_i$.

(2) $\quad \pi_i = p_i f_i'(C_i) - \bar{x}$,

where p_i is the price of manufactured goods in the ith industry in terms of grain. Equilibrium in the allocation of capital requires a uniform profit rate. That is,

(3) $\quad \pi_i = \pi_a$.

Since the profit rate in agriculture is specified to set the rate of return on capital for the whole economy, it follows that equalization of π_i and π_a is brought about by change in relative prices. Equalization of the profit rates is not necessarily realized during a single exchange period, however. It is useful at this point to distinguish between the classical concepts of "market price," which is determined by supply and demand, and "natural price," which is determined by cost of production. Ricardian natural price is a cost-of-production concept in which commodities exchange with one another according to the relative quantities of inputs used in the production of each. Accordingly, the natural price of the ith commodity may, with some simplification, be defined as the ratio of the marginal productivities of the composite factor employed. In terms of the model constructed here, in which grain is taken as numéraire, this would mean

(4) $\quad p_i^* = f_a'(C_a)/f_i'(C_i)$.

Since the amount of labor per unit of composite factor is assumed constant, the ratio of marginal productivities for the two commodities can also be viewed to express the "comparative quantity of labour which is necessary to their production."[10] Market price may diverge from natural price in the short run. When the two do diverge in a given industry, the profit rate in that industry diverges from the profit rate in the lead sector. In turn, it is this discrepancy in the profit rates that provides the basis for capital movements within the economy. An industry expands when market price exceeds natural price, contracts when market price is less than natural price, and remains stable when market price is equal to natural price. Capital thus enters, exits, or stays put in an industry depending whether that industry's market price is respectively greater than, less than, or equal to its natural price.

---

10. Ricardo, *op. cit.*, p. 48. This definition of natural price, which is derived from the equilibrium condition expressed in equation (3), involves certain simplifications, including the assumptions of a homogeneous labor force, a uniform composition for the composite factor over industries, a risk and uncertainty factor in all industries equal to that in agriculture, and no government taxes.

The allocation mechanism embodied in the uniform profit principle[11] is summarized in the following three equations:

(5) $p_i - p_i^* = e_i(C_i)$,

(6) $\pi_i - \pi_a = g_i(p_i - p_i^*)$, and

(7) $\Delta C_i = u_i(\pi_i - \pi_a)$.

Equation (5) defines the difference between market price and natural price in a given industry as a function of capital stock employed in that industry during the production period. It summarizes the demand-supply relations that exist within the ith commodity market. Equation (6) states that a divergence between market price and natural price gives rise to a disequilibrium profit rate in the industry. And equation (7) specifies the mechanism by which the stock of composite factor (i.e., capital) is adjusted in accord with profit maximization. General equilibrium prevails when all $\Delta C_i = 0$, which implies that the profit rate is identical in all industries and sectors of the economy.[12] At the same time, the criterion of uniform profitability implies that the market price is identical to the natural price in each industry.

Figures 3–5A through 3–5D give a graphic summary of the uniform profit principle. They show the way in which a uniform profit rate in the economy provides classical theory with the key criterion for identifying

---

11. Operation of the uniform profit principle is outlined in the following passages of Ricardo's *Principles*:

"It is then the desire, which every capitalist has, of diverting his funds from a less to a more profitable employment that prevents the market price of commodities from continuing for any length of time either much above or much below their natural price. It is this competition which so adjusts the changeable value of commodities that, after paying the wages for the labour necessary to their production, and all other expenses required to put the capital employed in its original state of efficiency, the remaining value or overplus will in each trade be in proportion to the value of the capital employed" (*ibid.*, p. 50).

"I have already remarked that the market price of a commodity may exceed its natural or necessary price, as it may be produced in less abundance than the new demand for it requires. This, however, is but a temporary effect. The high profits on capital employed in producing that commodity will naturally attract capital to that trade; and as soon as the requisite funds are supplied, and the quantity of the commodity is duly increased, its price will fall, and the profits of the trade will conform to the general level.... It is through the inequality of profits that capital is moved from one employment to another" (*ibid.*, p. 70).

12. The system is determinate. There are $4n + 1$ unknown (π_a, π_i, p_i, p_i^*, ΔC_i) and $4n + 1$ equations ((1), (2), (4), (5), and (7)). Parameters of the system include $\bar{x}$, and C; C_a is assumed pre-determined as a long-run function of C (see above, footnote 8); and the initial values of C_i are taken as given. Equation (6) is implied by equations (1), (2), and (4).

the vector of equilibrium relative prices. Starting with Figure 3–5A, we have the quantity of composite factor allocated to the agricultural sector (C_a) specified at a level to meet the demand for output as determined by the economy's population size, the established standard of living, and the magnitude of capital stock. This determines the profit rate for agriculture (π_a) which is stipulated to be *the* all-pervading profit rate for the entire economy in the sense that the rate of return to capital invested in each

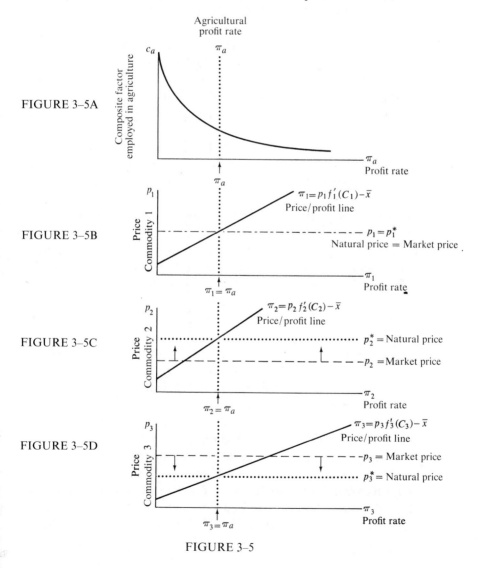

FIGURE 3–5A

FIGURE 3–5B

FIGURE 3–5C

FIGURE 3–5D

FIGURE 3–5

manufacturing industry must be identical to the rate of return established in the agricultural sector.

Figures 3–5B through 3–5D disaggregate the manufacturing sector into three industries. The profit-price function is drawn for each of these three industries in accord in with equation (2). Recall that profit is expressed in grain units per unit of composite factor and that relative prices are expressed as the price of a given commodity in terms of grain. Differences in the slope of the profit-price functions are due to differences in the marginal product of the composite factor in the various industries. The agricultural profit rate, set in Figure 3–5A, is projected downward by means of a dotted line. In order for equilibrium to prevail in the system, the uniform profit principle requires that those relative prices be established which are read off the profit-price functions at their respective intersections with the dotted general profit line. In the equilibrium condition in Figures 3–5A through 3–5D, $\pi_a = \pi_1 = \pi_2 = \pi_3$. Once this criterion is satisfied, market price equals natural price in each industry. In the short run the profit rate may not be uniform over all industries. Such a condition, as has already been noted, implies that market price is not equal to natural price in all industries. In order to demonstrate the short-run adjustments in graphic terms, a horizontal dashed line designating the initial short-run market price is drawn in each figure. In Figure 3–5B, the initial market price is already equal to the natural price of the industry, and the industry profit rate equals the profit rate in the lead sector. No change in capital stock allocated to this industry will occur. In Figure 3–5C, the initial market price is drawn less than the natural price. It follows that the industry's profit rate is less than that in agriculture, the lead sector. Capital will exit from the industry, the quantity of goods supplied to the market will drop, and market price will rise until equilibrium is established. Finally, in Figure 3–5D, the initial market price is drawn greater than the natural price. The industry's profit rate here exceeds the profit rate in the lead sector. Capital allocated to this industry will increase, the industry market price will fall as output expands, and equilibrium eventually is established when $\pi_3 = \pi_a$.

In sum, we note that the Ricardian use of the uniform profit principle provided a picture of long-run equilibrium prices. It was a theory, however, which could not handle the short run. It could say little about the set of relative prices that is determined in a single exchange period. If profit rates were not identical in all industries it was only possible to say that the uniform profit principle was not satisfied and that prices would change in the future. Nevertheless, the model does indicate that the adjustment trend would be in the direction of establishing equilibrium relative prices.

Marxist Prices

The classical theory of relative price determination is elaborated in some considerable detail by Karl Marx. Though Marx's analysis is fully structured within the framework of the uniform profit principle, it differs in a number of important respects from the Ricardian approach. Perhaps the most important difference is the absence of diminishing returns from the Marxist model: constant returns to scale in all industries is assumed. This means that the general profit rate for the economy at large is not linked, as in the Ricardian system, to a designated lead sector of the economy. For the Marxist model, the general profit rate is determined by the exploitation of labor and the size of the total capital stock. The exploitation of labor is the difference between the length of the working day (h) and the subsistence wage or "necessary labor time" (h^*), both expressed in hours. The total amount of surplus value generated by exploitation is the product of the number of laborers employed (N), and the hours of unpaid labor ($= N(h - h^*)$). Given the total stock of capital (K), expressed in hours of labor, in addition to specified values for N, h, and h^*, the general profit rate ($\bar{p}'$) is

(8) $\bar{p}' = N(h - h^*)/K.$

The general profit rate,[13] determined during the production period and introduced as a given into the exchange period, is the equilibrium rate of return to capital. It is toward this level that the profit rates in all individual industries (p_i') gravitate. The uniform profit principle specifies that a vector of equilibrium relative prices is established when the general profit rate prevails uniformly throughout the economy, i.e., when $p_i' = \bar{p}'$.

The general profit rate is to be distinguished from the internal profit rate for a given industry.[14] The internal profit rate (p_i') in the simplified

---

13. A detailed discussion of the rate of exploitation and the profit rate is contained in Chapter 7, especially sections III and IV.

14. The general profit rate is the weighted average of the specific internal rates of return on capital in the individual industries, that is, $\bar{p}' = \sum_1^n p_i' K_i / \sum_1^n K_i$, where $\bar{p}'$ is the general profit rate, p_i' is the profit rate internal to and K_i is the amount of capital employed in the ith industry.

Marxist analysis in which all capital employed is used up in the production process, is that percentage appreciation rate that equates the "cost price" (κ_i) with the "market price" (y_i). The cost price[15] per unit of output is the value of constant and variable capital inputs required to produce one unit of the ith commodity ($i = 1 \cdots n$). The commodity sells in exchange at a market price that includes a percentage mark-up over cost price.[16] Specifically,

(9) $\quad y_i = \kappa_i(1 + p_i')$.

The "price of production"[17] per unit of commodity in a given industry (y_i^*) is that price that specifies a mark-up percentage equal to the general profit rate. That is,

(10) $\quad y_i^* = \kappa_i(1 + \bar{p}')$.

The price of production is the commodity's long-run equilibrium exchange price. Market price, which is established by supply and demand,[18] may diverge from the price of production in the short run but corrective adjustments in the allocation of total capital stock and in industry output immediately takes place to force market price once again into equality with the price of production. Equilibrium prevails in any given industry when there is no tendency for capital stock to enter into or exit from the field of production. In these terms, the equilibrium mechanism is expressed in the following three equations:

(11) $\quad y_i - y_i^* = e_i(K_i)$,

---

15. Karl Marx, *op. cit.*, vol. III, pp. 26 and 163.

16. This relationship, which is restated in equation (9) immediately following in the text, is equivalent to that expressed above in equation (2) of Ricardo's system. The Ricardian equation specified profit as a value return per unit of composite factor, namely, $\pi_i = p_i f_i'(C_i) - \bar{x}$. By dividing each side of this equation first by $f_i'(C_i)$, profit is expressed per unit of commodity output, π_i^*. Next, by dividing each side of the equation by $\bar{x}^*(= \bar{x}/f_i'(C_i))$, profit per commodity is expressed as a rate return to capital employed per unit of output produced. Rearranging terms the equation becomes $p_i = \bar{x}^*(\pi_i^*/\bar{x}^* + 1)$, where $\bar{x}^*$ is the quantity of capital stock employed and consumed in the production process per unit of output and π_i^* is the profit return per unit of commodity output. Direct comparison of the Ricardian equation with the equivalent Marxist equation reveals that $p_i = y_i$, $\pi_i^*/\bar{x}^* = p_i'$, and $\bar{x}^* = \kappa$.

17. *Ibid.*, p. 194: "The price of production includes the average profit. We call it the price of production. It is really what Adam Smith calls *natural price*, and Ricardo calls *price of production*, or *cost of production*, and the physiocrats call *prix nécessaire*, because in the long run it is a prerequisite of supply, of the reproduction of commodities in every individual sphere."

18. Karl Marx, *op. cit.*, pp. 189–90.

(12) $p_i' - \bar{p}' = g_i(y_i - y_i^*)$, and

(13) $\Delta K_i = u_i(p_i' - \bar{p}')$

If, for whatever reasons (the pattern of commodity demand, perhaps), capital stock (K_i) in equation (11) is not optimally allocated, the composition of commodity output will not be ideal. The quantities supplied are then equated with demand at market prices that diverge from price of production,[19] that is, $(y_i - y_i^*) \neq 0$. As indicated by equation (12), the industry's internal rate of return on capital then diverges from the general profit rate, that is, $(p_i' - \bar{p}') \neq 0$. Since $g_i > 0$, a market price greater than the price of production implies an internal profit rate greater than the general profit rate. Additional capital is then attracted into the industry via equation (13). In the next period, capital stock in the industry is larger, output is greater, and the market price is lower. Adjustment continues in this manner from period to period until equilibrium is established as identified by the condition $p_i' = \bar{p}'$. The uniform profit principle thus appears in Marxist analysis as the basis for the equilibrating mechanism[20]

---

19. Consider the following passages by Marx concerning market price and price of production: "Hence, if supply and demand regulate the market-price, or rather the deviations of the market-price from the market-value [price of production], then, in turn, the market-value [price of production] regulates ... the centre round which fluctuations of supply and demand cause market-price to oscillate" (*ibid.*, p. 178).

"On the one hand, the relation of demand and supply, therefore, only explains the deviations of market-prices from market-values [price of production]. On the other, it explains the tendency to eliminate these deviations, i.e., to eliminate the effect of the relation of demand and supply.... For instance, if the demand, and consequently the market-price, fall, capital may be withdrawn, thus causing supply to shrink. It may also be that the market-value [price of production] itself shrinks and balances with the market-price as a result of inventions which reduce the necessary labour-time. Conversely, if the demand increases, and consequently the market-price rises above the market-value [price of production], this may lead to too much capital flowing into this line of production and production may swell to such an extent that the market-price will even fall below the market-value [price of production]" (*ibid.*, pp. 186–87).

20. *Ibid.*, pp. 191–92. "One sphere of production is, in fact, just as good or just as bad as another. Every one of them yields the same profit, and every one of them would be useless if the commodities it produced did not satisfy some social need .... Capital withdraws from a sphere with a low rate of profit and invades others, which yield a higher profit. Through this incessant outflow and influx, or, briefly, through its distribution among the various spheres, which depends on how the rate of profit falls here and rises there, it creates such a ratio of supply to demand that the average profit in the various spheres of production becomes the same, and values are, therefore, converted into prices of production.... The incessant equilibration of constant divergences is accomplished so much more quickly, 1) the more mobile the capital, i.e., the more easily it can be shifted from one sphere and from one place to another; 2) the more quickly labour-power can be transferred from one sphere to another and from one production locality to another."

in the adjustment of market price as well as the key criterion for identifying an equilibrium set of exchange prices.

Both sets of commodity prices—y_i and y_i^*—are expressed in time units of homogeneous labor power. In order to transform these sets of absolute prices into relative prices, it is necessary to select one commodity as numéraire and express relative prices in terms of the numéraire. Let us take the absolute price of the nth commodity as the numéraire and express relative market prices as

(14) $\quad z_i = y_i/y_n = (y_1/y_n, y_2/y_n, \ldots, y_{n-1}/y_n, 1)$,

and relative prices of production as

(15) $\quad z_i^* = y_i^*/y_n^* = (y_1^*/y_n^*, y_2^*/y_n^*, \ldots, y_{n-1}^*/y_n^*, 1)$.

Selection of the nth commodity as numéraire means that $z_n = z_n^* = 1$, which necessarily implies that $p_n' = \bar{p}'$ for the numéraire industry. With the substitution of relative prices for absolute prices, the Marxist price system may be summarized as follows:

(16) $\quad z_i = \kappa_i(1 + p_i')/y_n$,

(17) $\quad z_i^* = \kappa_i(1 + \bar{p}')/y_n^*$,

(18) $\quad z_i - z_i^* = e_i(K_i)$,

(19) $\quad p_i' - \bar{p}' = g_i(z_i - z_i^*)$, and

(20) $\quad \Delta K_i = u_i(p_i' - \bar{p}')$.

The system is determinate. In addition to the $2n + 3$ given parameters $(\kappa_i, K_i, \bar{p}', y_n, y_n^*)$, there are $4n - 2$ unknowns $(p_i', \Delta K_i, z_i, z_i^*)$, and $4n - 2$ relationships (equations (16), (17), (18), and (20)—with one relationship for the numéraire commodity deleted from each of equations (16) and (17), while equation (19) is implied by equations (16) and (17)). If a uniform profit rate prevails in the system, relative prices are identified to be in equilibrium. Market price equals price of production in every industry and capital is optimally allocated.

The mechanism of the uniform profit principle is presented graphically in Figures 3–6A through 3–6C. Each diagram depicts a given industry. The internal profit rate is measured on the horizontal axis and the general profit rate is introduced as a dotted vertical line passing through each of the three diagrams. The points of intersection between the dotted general profit rate line and each of the upward-sloping profit-price functions drawn in each figure indicate the respective equilibrium relative prices for each industry. At these points the internal profit rate equals the general profit rate and the market price equals the price of production. The initial market price is drawn as a dashed line in each diagram. In Figure 3–6A, equilibrium prevails at the outset. In Figure 3–6B, the internal profit rate which corresponds to the initial market price is lower than the general rate. Capital exits from the industry, output falls, market price is raised in subsequent periods, and equilibrium is ultimately established. In Figure

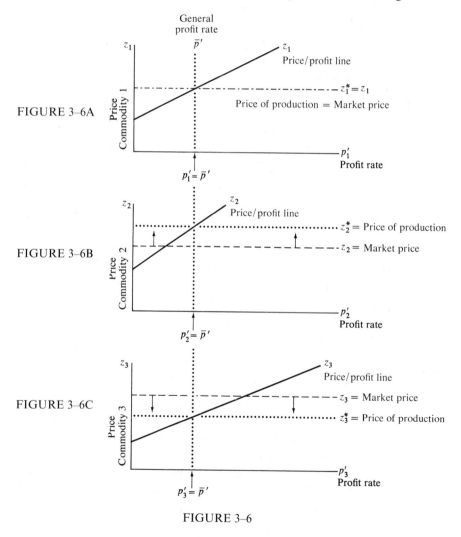

FIGURE 3–6A

FIGURE 3–6B

FIGURE 3–6C

FIGURE 3–6

3–6C, the opposite situation prevails at the outset, namely, the initial market price dictates an internal profit rate that is higher than the general rate. Capital enters the industry, output increases, market price falls, and in some future time period equilibrium is established. If a uniform profit rate does not prevail, the system is not in equilibrium. Once a uniform profit rate is obtained, however, relative prices are in equilibrium for the entire economy.

Conclusion

As has been noted, commodity prices are determined in the basic classical model during the exchange period. We know that the supplies of commodities placed on the market are those manufactured during the just-completed production period. Each commodity market is cleared—at some price. What has been called here the uniform profit principle is the analytical construct that provides classical economics with an answer to the query as to how commodity prices move once relative scarcity has determined commodity prices in a single exchange period. The uniform profit principle attempts two main tasks: first, it sets down a criterion for identifying an equilibrium set of relative prices for commodities; and second, it provides a mechanism that would automatically move short-run disequilibrium commodity prices toward long-run equilibrium levels. The uniform profit principle is thus yet another building block in classical analysis that illustrates how capital is structured as the key variable in classical economic theory. The uniform profit principle approach to relative price determination probably reached its zenith in the 1860's. With the emergence of marginal utility analysis, scientific inquiry shifted to demand-theoretical investigations of the basis for equilibrium in the commodity market. Walrasian general equilibrium analysis became the new analytical frontier.

VI. Determinants of Capital Accumulation

Capital was not only the dominant theoretical construct of classical theory; it was also the key variable for achieving the major policy objective of classical economics, namely, economic growth. In terms of classical analysis, output is a function of capital—commodities are produced by means of commodities. Accordingly, capital and economic growth are inextricably intertwined. If the level of production is to be raised, the quantity of inputs must be increased. Thus, to account for economic growth, we need explain the determinants of capital accumulation.

The economy's net product (= total commodity output less replacement of variable capital and depreciated fixed capital) is the resource base for saving.[21] Considered as income, the net product is divided between the capitalists' profits and the landlords' rents. Considered as expenditure, the net product is divided between "productive" and "unproductive" purposes. The part of the net product allocated to investment represents "productive consumption" in the sense that it is used to produce other commodities. The remaining part of the net product is used as a source of immediate satisfaction and represents "unproductive consumption" inasmuch as it is not used to produce commodities. Likewise, resources spent in support of productive labor yields a material commodity output while resources spent in support of unproductive labor yields only services which do not have material form. Saving constitutes that portion of the net product that is not consumed unproductively by the original recipients of the net product. It thus represents the income earner's decision to abstain from the immediate enjoyment derived from unproductive commodity consumption. Of total saving, one portion is invested directly, that is to say, allocated to capital accumulation by internal or equity financing; a second portion is channeled to the loanable funds market where it is then borrowed for (a) debt-financed investment and (b) debt-financed unproductive consumption. It follows that while all investment originates in saving, not all saving is invested. In terms of classical analysis, saving is equal to investment only if debt-financed unproductive consumption is zero.

From the principle which Nassau Senior called "abstinence"[22] evolved the classical theory of the role of the interest rate in the decision of income

---

21. John Stuart Mill, *op. cit.,* pp. 163–64: "The fund from which saving can be made, is the surplus of the produce of labour, after supplying the necessaries of life to all concerned in production: including those employed in replacing the materials, and keeping the fixed capital in repair. More than this surplus cannot be saved under any circumstances. As much as this, though it never is saved, always might be. This surplus is the fund from which the enjoyments, as distinguished from the necessaries, of the producers are provided; it is the fund from which all are subsisted, who are not themselves engaged in production; and from which all additions are made to capital."

22. Nassau W. Senior, *An Outline of the Science of Political Economy* (1836), New York: Augustus M. Kelley, 1965, p. 58: "*Abstinence:* a term by which we express the conduct of a person who either abstains from the unproductive use of what he can command, or designedly prefers the production of remote to that of immediate results."

recipients to abstain from current unproductive consumption in lieu of payment for abstinence.[23] The classical discussion employed the interest rate as the independent variable in a model that explains the initial division of the net product between saving and consumption as well as its ultimate division between investment (productive consumption) and unproductive consumption. The total net product of the economy is not, of course, loaned and borrowed on the market. Recipients of the net product invest and consume part of the pie themselves. The remainder they supply to the loanable funds market where, at the equilibrium rate of interest, the excess supplies and excess demands of all individual market transactors sum to zero. In the loanable funds market, the demand for loans is derived from (a) investment demand generated by capitalists and entrepreneurs, and (b) unproductive consumption demand generated by government and some private individuals.[24] Supply of and demand for funds on the market then determine the interest rate. In order to give proper perspective to the allocative function of the interest rate within classical economics, main attention need be focused on the aggregate division of the net product.

The following set of equations summarizes the main relationships:

(1) $S(i) = Z - C,$

(2) $Z = P + U,$

23. John Stuart Mill, *op. cit.:* "As the wages of the labourer are the remuneration of labour, so the profits of the capitalist are properly, according to Mr. Senior's well-chosen expression, the remuneration of abstinence. They are what he gains by forbearing to consume his capital for his own uses, and allowing it to be consumed by productive labourers for their uses. For this forbearance he requires a recompense" (p. 405).

"The gross profits from capital, the gains returned to those who supply the funds for production, must suffice for these three purposes. They must afford a sufficient equivalent for abstinence, indemity for risk, and remuneration for the labour and skill required for superintendence. These different compensations may be either paid to the same, or to different persons. The capital, or some part of it, may be borrowed: may belong to someone who does not undertake the risks or the trouble of the business. In that case, the lender or owner is the person who practices the abstinence; and is remunerated for it by the interest paid to him, while the difference between the interest and the gross profits remunerates the exertions and risks of the undertaker" (p. 406).

24. *Ibid.*, p. 638: "We will suppose commerce to be in a quiescent condition, no employment being unusually prosperous, and none particularly distressed. In these circumstances, the more thriving producers and traders have their capital fully employed, and many are able to transact business to a considerably greater extent than they have capital for. These are naturally borrowers: and the amount which they desire to borrow, and can obtain credit for, constitutes the demand for loans on account of productive employment. To these must be added the loans required by Government, and by landowners, or other unproductive consumers who have good security to give. This constitutes the mass of loans for which there is an habitual demand."

(3) $P = I_1(i) + I_2(i),$

(4) $U = C + B(i),$

(5) $S(i) = I_1(i) + I_2(i) + B(i),$

(6) $S(i) - I_1(i) = I_2(i) + B(i).$

All magnitudes are expressed in money terms with commodity prices assumed constant. Equation (1) states the division of the given net product, Z, in accord with the initial decision to abstain, $S(i)$, or not to abstain, C, from immediate unproductive consumption. Here the interest rate (i) is the intervening variable. Equation (2) specifies that the net product is consumed either productively (P) or unproductively (U). To be consumed productively, resources must be added to total capital stock. As equation (3) indicates, this investment demand is generated through internal or equity financing, $I_1(i)$, and/or through credit financing, $I_2(i)$. In a parallel fashion in equation (4), unproductive consumption, C, is taken out of net product received as income or originates in borrowed funds, $B(i)$. A chain of substitutions of equations (3) and (4) into equation (2) followed by substitution of the resulting expression for Z into equation (1) yields equation (5) which summarizes the equilibrium condition in the system. Specifically, the resources set aside out of net product by abstinence are absorbed by capital investment and by unproductive consumption loans. There is a unique interest rate established at which the system is in equilibrium. At this equilibrium interest rate, the level of investment— and hence the rate of economic expansion—is determined. The loanable funds market is summarized by equation (6). The left side of the equation is a measure of the supply of resources placed on the loanable funds market ($=$ total abstinence minus equity financed investment), while the right side of the equation is the demand for credit for both productive and unproductive purposes. Here, $S'(i)>0$ and $I_1'(i)$, $I_2'(i)$, $B'(i)<0$.

In Figure 3–7 total net product (Z) is measured as the base of the diagram. Saving (S), investment (I), and deficit-financed unproductive consumption (B) are each measured from the left, while unproductive consumption out of income (C) is measured from the right. Magnitudes are denominated in money terms with commodity prices assumed. The $S + C$ schedule indicates the division of the net product as a function of the interest rate (i). Abstinence is the decision to forego unproductive consumption and interest is paid to reward or compensate those who surrender their current command over resources. The positive slope of the $S + C$ schedule indicates that the degree of sacrifice associated with abstinence increases as saving increases and as unproductive consumption decreases relative to the total net product. Viewed from left to right in the diagram, the $S + C$ schedule may be considered conveniently as the supply of loanable funds schedule. Of these resources, one portion (I_1) is demanded for internal or equity-financed investment, a second portion (I_2) represents the loan-demand for investment funds, and a third portion (B) represents the loan-demand for unproductive consumption by government and private individuals. Total investment demand for resources is drawn in Figure 3–7 as the I schedule, where $I = I_1 + I_2$. The total demand for investment and for unproductive consumption goods is drawn in Figure 3–7 as the $I + B$ schedule. All these schedules are negative functions of the interest rate. Intersection of the $I + B$ and $S + C$ schedules determines the equilibrium rate of interest for the economy. At this interest rate (indicated by the horizontal dotted line in Figure 3–7) the quantity of resources invested is $O_1 Z_1$, and the quantity of resources consumed unproductively is $O_2 Z_1$, of which $Z_1 Z_2$ is the quantity of resources borrowed on the market for unproductive consumption purposes. It is in this way that the interest rate serves to determine the level of investment and rate of capital accumulation. The position and slope of the I schedule depends upon the pro-

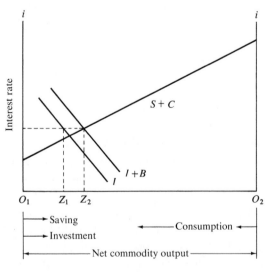

FIGURE 3–7

ductivity return of investment. Technological change that increases the productivity of new capital, i.e., increases the ratio of commodity outputs to commodity inputs, will also affect the demand for investment. Specifically, the *I* schedule in Figure 3–7 would shift to the right, thereby tending to raise the level of investment and speed the rate of capital accumulation. Foreign-trade policy, especially with regard to food imports, is also significant in this context. Classical theory presumed that opening the economy to tariff-free importation of cheap foreign foodstuffs would have two main effects: first, money wages would fall, the general profit rate would rise as the net product was increased, and the inducement to invest would increase; second, capital would shift out of domestic agriculture and rent's relative share of the net product would be reduced.[25]

Once the investment schedule is specified, the equilibrium interest rate established by the intersection of the *I* + *B* and *S* + *C* schedules determines the level of investment. Anything that raises the equilibrium interest rate (such as an increased demand for debt-financed unproductive consumption by government)[26] discourages investment and reduces the rate of capital accumulation. This can be envisioned in terms of Figure 3–7 by supposing a rightward shift in the *I* + *B* schedule due exclusively to a shift in *B*. In addition, the model implies that capital accumulation also can be discouraged by taxation. To the extent that government taxes have their incidence on the net product, they shorten the base of Figure 3–7, shift the

---

25. To the extent that the propensity for abstinence from unproductive consumption is lower for the landlord class than the capitalist class, changes in the distribution of income affects the equilibrium interest rate. Because landlords are viewed to be prodigal in their expenditures, an increase in the relative rent share would cause an upward shift and/or clockwise rotation (from the right axis) in the *S* + *C* schedule in Figure 3–7. The effect of this shift would be to raise the equilibrium rate of interest, reduce the level of investment, and contribute to an earlier arrival of the stationary state. Conversely, reduction of the relative rent share due to a technological advance in agriculture would cause a downward shift and/or counterclockwise rotation (from the right axis) in the *S* + *C* schedule in Figure 3–7. Accompanying this change would be a lowering of the equilibrium rate of interest and an increase in the level of investment.

26. Mill writes (*op. cit.*, p. 643): "A time of war, for example, is a period of unusual drafts on the loan market. The Government, at such times, generally incurs new loans, and as these usually succeed each other rapidly as long as the war lasts, the general rate of interest is kept higher in war than in peace, without reference to the rate of profit, and the productive industry is stinted of its usual supplies.... The same effect on interest which is produced by Government loans for war expenditure, is produced by the sudden opening of any new and generally attractive mode of permanent investment. The only instance of this kind in recent history on a scale comparable to that of the war loans, is the absorption of capital in the construction of railways."

left axis rightward, and *ceteris paribus* push the $I + B$ schedule rightward by an equal distance. The $I + B$ schedule then intersects the $S + C$ schedule at a higher interest rate and at a correspondingly lower level of investment.[27] What classical economists termed the "stationary state"[28] is the ultimate in the discouragement of investment. A significant theory describing the path toward the stationary state was offered by David Ricardo. In Ricardo's model,[29] a closed economy is constructed which is specified to have a fixed amount of arable land and diminishing returns in agriculture. As capital accumulates in this system, the profit rate in agriculture falls. Because agriculture is the lead sector, the decline is then spread to the rest of the economy. In graphic terms the diminishing productivity of capital in Ricardian analysis can be translated as a leftward shift in the investment schedule in Figure 3–7. The stationary state is established once the I schedule intersects the vertical axis on the left at the equilibrium rate of interest, i.e., when investment demand is zero at the prevailing rate of interest. At this point the profit rate is termed to be at its minimum acceptable level. It is a zero growth situation.

27. Although J. S. Mill recognized that "There is no tax which is not partly paid from what would otherwise have been saved" (*ibid.*, p. 821), he did not regard taxes to be as injurious to the economy as government debt. Apparently underlying this viewpoint is an implicit assumption that the saving of the tax payer is not reduced by the full amount of the tax because the tax levy is accompanied by a concurrent increase in abstinence.

28. *Ibid.*, p. 172: "When a country has carried production as far as in the existing state of knowledge it can be carried with an amount of return corresponding to the average strength of the effective desire of accumulation in that country, it has reached what is called the stationary state; the state in which no further addition will be made to capital unless there takes place either some improvement in the arts of production, or an increase in the strength of the desire to accumulate."

29. The Ricardian model of relative income shares (David Ricardo, *op. cit.*, chapters 2, 5, 6) can be treated in its essentials as a single-sector agricultural economy. Ricardo abridged the classical question of the determinants of the division of total capital stock between fixed and variable capital by specifiying a composite factor of production composed of machinery and labor in fixed proportion. Agricultural output (Q_a), denominated in grain units, is then defined as a function of a fixed quantity of land and a variable quantity of composite factor (C_a). The total production function is then expressed $Q_a = f_a(C_a)$. Diminishing returns to the composite factor is assumed, that is, $f_a'' < 0$. Of the total output, the composite factor receives its marginal product ($= C_a[f_a'(C_a)]$) and the remainder of total product is paid as rent (R), that is, $R = f_a(C_a) - C_a[f_a'(C_a)]$. The relative share of total output going to rent is $R/Q_a = 1 - C_a[f_a'(C_a)]/f_a(C_a) = 1 - f_a'(C_a)/g(C_a) = 1 - \varepsilon$, where $g(C_a)$ is the average product of the composite factor ($= [f_a(C_a)]/C_a$), and ε is the elasticity of the production function with respect to the variable factor ($= \Delta Q_a C_a/Q_a \Delta C_a$). Whereas the assumption of diminishing returns means that $\varepsilon < 1$, an upward trend in the relative rent share, as specified by Ricardo, requires that ε decrease as more of the composite factor is employed, that is, $d\varepsilon/dC_a < 0$. The latter specification of the production function is given in Ricardo's own numerical example of production relations. (Cf. H. Barkai, "Ricardo on Factor Prices and Income Distribution in a Growing Economy," *Economica*, August 1959, pp. 245–46.)

In summary, then, the pace of capital accumulation is increased by (1) an increase in abstinence; (2) technological change that increases the productivity of capital and gives a fillip to the propensity to invest; (3) a reduction of government expenditures, whether debt-financed or tax-financed; and (4) a reduction in the relative price of foodstuffs brought about either through abolition of the tariff on food imports or by means of technological advances in domestic agriculture.

VII. Capital and Population Growth

Classical analysis of economic expansion was necessarily incomplete without a demographic theory to explain population growth. Although the production of commodities is defined to be a function of commodity inputs, ultimate production activity in classical theory requires that one portion of commodity capital (i.e., variable capital) be transformed into labor power before production activity begins. Before the time that the wheels of production start turning, capitalists must assemble machines and labor in the proportion dictated by technology. The labor-machine ratio (α), which enters so prominently in the discussion of the basic classical model (see section I of this chapter), is a technologically determined parameter. Though classical economists recognized the importance of technological change, the labor-machine ratio was typically treated as a parametric given. The usual approach was to view the ratio as exogenous to the basic model. Only Karl Marx came to grips with the problem of devising a theory with which to account for changes in the parameter.

Whatever the value of the labor-machine ratio, it is clear that any increase in the level of production requires that both more machines *and* more labor be employed. Any explanation of economic growth, therefore, that did not provide for concurrent growth in the number of machines and men was necessarily incomplete, to say the very least. Because capital stood as the key variable in classical economics, it was encumbent upon classical analysis to show that capital accumulation was both a necessary as well as a sufficient condition for economic growth. The classical population equation made this possible.

Classical population theory rests on an assumption that working-class households have a target per-capita real income[30] which is maintained

---

30. Let y = the target per-capita household income, e = the number of income earners per household, and n = the number of persons in the average household (i.e., desired family size). The subsistence rate ($\bar{w}$) may then be expressed as $\bar{w} = yn/e$. The use of $\bar{w}$ as the measure of the subsistence level thus assumes not only that the household's target per-capita income (y) is given, but so are the parameters of household organization (e and n).

over the long run, generally with an upward trend for the population at large. The so-called "subsistence" wage rate in classical theory designated the long-run supply price of labor. It is essentially an historically determined parameter of the system and is responsive to realized changes in the household's consumption level. As householders become accustomed to consuming luxury commodities, the previously unfamiliar goods become commonplace and what was once considered a superfluous frill becomes viewed as an indispensable necessity. In the short run, however, the subsistence wage is relatively stable. When the market wage (w), therefore, exceeds the subsistence wage ($\overline{w}$), households do not immediately raise their per-capita standard of consumption. Instead, the improved income situation prompts an increase in the population. That is, in terms of the classical population equation,

(1) $\quad \Delta N^s = f(w - \overline{w})$,

where the labor supply (N^s) is assumed to be a constant proportion of the population. The subsistence wage is a loosely constructed heuristic device. Functionally, it was a measure of the average cost per time period to maintain the stock of labor. In this respect it was identical to the classical notion of "natural price": When market wage exceeds the subsistence wage, population increases; when the market wage is equal to the subsistence wage, population remains unchanged; and when market wage is less than the subsistence wage, population decreases.[31] Householders, in their decisions to produce people, were thus asserted to respond to price stimuli in a manner identical to capitalists in their decisions to produce commodities. Growth of the labor supply is thus set by economic determinants. Here the key independent variable is capital accumulation. As was discussed above in section II of this chapter, an increase in total capital stock increases the demand for labor. The market wage rises

---

31. In this connection David Ricardo writes: "Labour, like all other things which are purchased and sold, and which may be increased or diminished in quantity, has its natural and its market price. The natural price of labour is that price which is necessary to enable the labourers, one with another, to subsist and to perpetuate their race, without either increase or diminution" (*op. cit.*, p. 52).

"It is when the market price of labour exceeds its natural price that the condition of the labourer is flourishing and happy, that he has it in his power to command a greater proportion of the necessaries and enjoyments of life, and therefore to rear a healthy and numerous family. When, however, by the encouragement which high wages give to the increase of population, the number of labourers is increased, wages again fall to their natural price, and indeed from a reaction sometimes fall below it" (*ibid.*, p. 53).

because the short-run labor supply cannot increase. Over the longer run, however, population and the work force do increase. As long as capital accumulation is positive, the demand for labor schedule in Figure 3–3 is shifting upward and the market wage is held above the subsistence wage. This relation is readily summarized as follows:

(2) $(w - \bar{w}) = g(\Delta K)$.

As represented in terms of equations (1) and (2), classical population theory ties growth in the labor supply directly to capital accumulation. The theory demonstrates that capital accumulation is both a necessary as well as a sufficient condition for economic expansion. While the classical population theory had the effect of making demographic issues an admissable subject within the ambit of economics, classical economists attempted little in the way of serious demographic theory. For them, the vital challenge had already been met. Not until theories of technological change (e.g., Karl Marx) and factor substitution (e.g., marginal productivity theory) were developed to demonstrate that the population equation can be replaced by an equation of technological change and that machinery can be systematically substituted for labor did economists' concern for demographic variables fade away. As long as the classical approach was dominant, population theory was an indispensable adjunct to economic analysis.

The Analytical Role 4
of Money in Classical Theory

Classical economics revolutionized the analytical importance assigned to the money supply variable. Money was pushed from the central place it held in the analysis of latter-day mercantilism. The Quesnaysian Revolution first deleted money from the list of the determinants of the level of aggregate demand. And, in the formative years of classical economics, the theoretical role of the money supply was worked out in sufficient detail to refute mercantilist theory and to ridicule mercantilist policy recommendations.

I. The Quesnaysian Model: Omission of Money as a Key Variable

Considered from the viewpoint that "it takes a theory to kill a theory," the Cantillon-Quesnay aggregate demand theory may be interpreted as part of a broader analytical attack on the dominant latter-day mercantilist view that "money matters." On the demand side, the Cantillon-Quesnay approach developed what might be characterized as a "real," as opposed to a monetary, theory of aggregate demand by its emphasis on expenditure multipliers and an autonomous expenditure component, namely, rent. The thrust of the demand argument is clearly discernible: the money supply does not matter. It is, however, from the supply side that the main Quesnaysian-Classical attack on the monetarist position of latter-day mercantilism was launched. With aggregate output defined to be a function of the nation's capital stock, Quesnay's model pointed to the fact that output depends on real inputs. Quesnay's analysis—and, with few exceptions the analysis of the other classical economists who succeeded him—indicated no way in which the money supply could influence output. It would appear then that Quesnay's foundations for classical economics specified no role for money on either the demand or the supply side of the model. As is revealed by a review of Quesnay's system (Chapter 2, section II), the money supply is conspicuous by its absence.

II. "Money Doesn't Matter": The Price-Specie-Flow Doctrine

The Mercantilist Approach: David Hume

The price-specie-flow doctrine, frequently regarded as the analytical advance that gave the *coup de grâce* to mercantilism, is especially significant for the passive role that it assigns to the money supply. It rejects the mercantilist view that the money supply can influence the level of aggregate demand, and, thereby, employment and output. It asserts that the money supply determines the price level alone. Briefly stated, the specie-flow doctrine emphasizes that "money doesn't matter" by demonstrating that each country will automatically obtain the supply of specie it needs. The money supply would thus take care of itself and those policies designed to assure a favorable balance of payments were misdirected.

The main components of the specie-flow doctrine may be delineated as follows: (a) each country operates on a specie monetary standard: (b) the price level in each country is determined by the money supply; (c) balance of payments for each country is a function of relative price levels in trading countries; and (d) international balances of payments are paid in specie. David Hume is traditionally recognized to have written the first or the most influential statement of the price-specie-flow doctrine, bringing together all of these analytical building blocks that constitute the theory.[1] Hume's formulation of the specie-flow doctrine is worked out in an essentially mercantilistic theoretical framework. Hume's analysis is not that of classical economics. His aggregate demand function is that of the latter-day mercantilists—that is, $D = f(M^s)$. But his conception of aggregate supply assumes a special full-employment case of the mercantilist supply function—that is, $S = \phi(P, U, w)$. In other words, Hume's argument that changes in the money supply have their impact almost

---

1. David Hume, "Of the Balance of Trade," (1752). Contained in *Early Economic Thought* (E. A. Monroe, editor), Cambridge: Harvard University Press, 1924, pp. 323–38.

exclusively on prices is advanced by assertion or assumption and not by analysis. His assumption of near full employment ($U \simeq 0$) is an empirical assertion concerning the main independent variable of the mercantilist supply equation; it is not a statement that disputes the mercantilist analytical framework. Hume's essay, though it seriously questions mercantilist policy, develops no new alternative theory. It is unlikely that the specie-flow argument could have gained any wide acceptance had the Quesnaysian Revolution not taken place. Hume's essay would likely have met the same fate of benign neglect as Isaac Gervaise's account of the self-regulating mechanism for distributing the world's specie supply among the nations of the world. It was the emergence of classical economics that provided a radically new theory of aggregate supply, defining output as a function of previously accumulated capital stock, emphasizing that commodities are produced essentially by means of commodities, and indicating that changes in the nation's money supply have no impact on the nation's productive capacity or output. Classical theory provided the analytical basis for the specie-flow doctrine. It is therefore appropriate to consider a classical economist such as Adam Smith—and not a mercantilist such as David Hume—as the specie-flow slayer of the mercantilist monetary dragon.

The Classical Approach: Adam Smith
That Adam Smith was well acquainted with David Hume's conceptualization of the specie-flow mechanism is documented by the concise summary of Hume's doctrine set down in Smith's *Lectures on Police, Justice, Revenue and Arms.*[2] It is noteworthy, however, that even at this early date (1763) Smith was critical of Hume's position. Specifically, Smith accused Hume of having "gone a little into the notion that public opulence consists in money."[3] Quite possibly Smith objected to Hume's contention that an increase in the money supply would cause, initially at least, an increase in output. In the *Lectures* Smith insisted that society's output of goods was independent of the nation's money supply. In the *Wealth of Nations* he elaborated the same point in further detail. Smith's fundamental proposition that "money is not wealth" constituted his basic polemic against

---

2. Adam Smith, *Lectures on Justice, Police, Revenue and Arms.* Reported by a student in 1763. Edited with an introduction and notes by Edwin Cannan (1896), New York, 1964.
3. *Ibid.,* p. 197.

mercantilist doctrines. For the most part, however, Smith posed this particular argument against a mercantilist strawman of his own construction. What he lacked in 1763 in his attack on mercantilist analysis was (1) a theory of aggregate demand that clearly excluded the money supply as an independent variable and (2) a theory of aggregate supply in which the independent variable was unaffected by changes in the money supply. The Quesnaysian Revolution, which had its impact on Smith after 1763, suggested solutions to both problems. Quesnay's basic model refuted the mercantilist contention that aggregate demand depends on the money supply and, as far as his followers were concerned, laid the whole to rest. In addition, Quesnay specified output to be a function of capital stock.

Adam Smith's discussion of the "extent of the market"[4] suggests an awareness of the relevance of the level of aggregate demand to the growth theory of the *Wealth of Nations*. But concentrating his attention, as he did, on the supply side of his model, Smith neglected the demand side. What statements appear in the *Wealth of Nations* on the question of demand are tentative in nature. Smith made no attempt to develop fully the demand side of his theoretical structure. Nevertheless, in his discussion of capital, Smith indicated that an insufficient domestic demand for the nation's output presents no problem. He argued that the international market consisted of the reciprocal demands of nations for one another's surpluses. Whenever a portion of a nation's output was not absorbed in the domestic market, capital investment would move into the foreign trade sector to seek markets abroad, thereby relieving the country of unwanted surpluses and bringing in their place goods "for which there is a demand."[5] This line of reasoning—suggestive of a rudimentary Say's Law—permitted Smith to argue that the level of aggregate demand was sufficient, in the long run, to guarantee a fully employed economy.[6] In addition, it enabled him to

---

4. Adam Smith, *The Wealth of Nations*, New York: Modern Library Edition, 1937, pp. 17ff.

5. *Ibid.*, p. 353: "When the produce of any particular branch of industry exceeds what the demand of the country requires, the surplus must be sent abroad, and exchanged for something for which there is a demand at home."

6. *Ibid.*, p. 354: "The extent of the home-trade and of the capital which can be employed in it, is necessarily limited by the value of the surplus produce of all those distant places within the country which have occasion to exchange their respective productions with one another. That of the foreign trade of consumption, by the value of the surplus produce of the whole country and of what can be purchased with it. That of the carrying trade, by the value of the surplus produce of all the different countries in the world. Its possible extent, therefore, is in a manner infinite in comparison of that of the other two, and is capable of absorbing the greatest capitals."

argue, in yet another context, that no mercantilist governmental measure should be taken to favor foreign trade over any other branch of economic activity.

A set of circumstances in which the money supply can influence aggregate demand for a country's output was recognized by Smith in his discussion of the mercantile system. If, due to a maldistribution of specie, the price level in one country were out of line with world prices, Smith indicated that changes would occur in the level of economic activity and employment in that country.[7] The qualifications that Smith imposed, however, are particularly significant. Smith pointed to a nation's "political institutions" as the root cause for a non-optimum specie supply with its adverse effects. Spain and Portugal, the two countries he singled out, had prevented (by taxation and export prohibitions) the establishment of a free market for specie.[8] One is left to infer from Smith's discussion that no ill effects would occur if specie were allowed to move in a free market. Instead of major price and employment adjustments (as would be required in the

---

7. Cf. the following passages: "But that degradation in the value of silver which, being the effect either of the peculiar situation, or of the political institutions of a particular country, takes place only in that country, is a matter of very great consequence, which, far from tending to make any body really richer, tends to make every body really poorer. The rise in the money price of all commodities, which is in this case peculiar to that country, tends to discourage more or less every sort of industry which is carried on within it, and to enable foreign nations, by furnishing almost all sorts of goods for a smaller quantity of silver than its own workmen can afford to do, to undersell them, not only in the foreign, but even in the home market" (*ibid.*, p. 478). "The cheapness of gold and silver, or what is the same thing, the dearness of all commodities, which is the necessary effect of this redundancy of the precious metals, discourages both the agriculture and the manufacturers of Spain and Portugal, and enables foreign nations to supply them with many sorts of rude, and with almost all sorts of manufactured produce, for a smaller quantity of gold and silver than what they themselves can either raise or make them for at home" (*ibid.*, p. 479).

8. *Ibid.*, pp. 478–79: "It is the peculiar situation of Spain and Portugal as proprietors of the mines, to be the distributors of gold and silver to all the other countries of Europe. Those metals ought naturally, therefore, to be somewhat cheaper in Spain and Portugal than in any other part of Europe. The difference, however, should be no more than the amount of the freight and insurance....Spain by taxing, and Portugal by prohibiting the exportation of gold and silver, load that exportation with the expense of smuggling, and raise the value of those metals in other countries so much above what it is in their own, by the whole amount of this expense....The tax and prohibition operate in two different ways. They not only lower very much the value of the previous metals in Spain and Portugal, but by detaining there a certain quantity of those metals which would otherwise flow over other countries, they keep up their value in those other countries somewhat above what it otherwise would be, and thereby give those countries a double advantage in their commerce with Spain and Portugal. ...Remove the tax and the prohibition, and as the quantity of gold and silver will diminish considerably in Spain and Portugal, so it will increase somewhat in other countries and the value of those metals, their proportion to the annual produce of land and labour, will soon come to a level, or very near to a level, in all."

case of Spain and Portugal), the free market in specie would make small, marginal adjustments in the nation's economy without any noticeable effect on the level of economic activity. In the absence of market imperfections, therefore, the money supply would not influence the level of aggregate demand.

Smith's formulation of the specie-flow mechanism is rather elegant in its simplicity. To begin with, Smith assumed the existence of an international purchasing-power parity for the monetary metals. The market for the precious metals, as viewed by Smith, is the broadest based, most developed, and most competitive market that exists for any commodity. Whenever and wherever the local price of specie in terms of commodities diverges from the international purchasing-power parity, specie movements take place immediately.[9] The world demand for specie thus appears to an individual nation as infinitely elastic with respect to its price in terms of commodities. Any small deviation in the domestic commodity price of specie from the international parity results in immediate specie export (or import). Smith's discussion of the adjustment mechanism very closely resembles the specie-flow mechanism described by later classical economists, except for the fact that Smith focused on the specie market and the commodity price of specie rather than on the commodity markets and the specie price of commodities.

Smith's model spells out the demand for and supply of specie as well as the short-run and long-run equilibrium conditions of the specie market. The quantity of specie demanded, A^d, is some (constant) function, v, of the

---

9. *Ibid.*, p. 404: "No commodities regulate themselves more easily or more exactly according to this effectual demand than gold and silver; because, on account of the small bulk and great value of those metals, no commodities can be more easily transported from one place to another, from the places where they are cheap, to those where they are dear, from the places where they exceed, to those where they fall short of this effectual demand.... When the quantity of gold and silver imported into any country exceeds the effectual demand, no vigilance of government can prevent their exportation. All the sanguinary laws of Spain and Portugal are not able to keep their gold and silver at home. The continual importations from Peru and Brazil exceed the effectual demand of those countries, and sink the price of those metals there below that in the neighbouring countries. If, on the contrary, in any particular country their quantity fell short of the effectual demand, so as to raise their price above that of the neighbouring countries, the government would have no occasion to take any pains to import them."

Smith goes on to describe the stability in the commodity price of specie in the following manner (*ibid.*, p. 405): "It is partly owing to the easy transportation of gold and silver from the places where they abound to those where they are wanted, that the price of those metals does not fluctuate continually like that of the greater part of other commodities, which are hindered by their bulk from shifting their situation, when the market happens to be either over or understocked with them."

supply of commodities, Q^s, and the price of specie in terms of commodities, p. That is,

(1) $\quad A^d = \dfrac{vQ^s}{p}.$

In terms of classical theory, aggregate commodity output is a function of the nation's given total capital stock:

(2) $\quad Q^s = \Psi(K).$

This last relationship is of crucial importance since it provides the needed analytical explanation of the determinants of commodity output. It indicates that output is independent of the money supply. Substituting (2) into (1) yields a determinant demand-for-specie function in which the value for Q^s is explained rather than assumed. The supply of specie in the country is determined by the nation's past history:

(3) $\quad A^s = \bar{A}^s.$

Equilibrium is then established when

(4) $\quad A^s = A^d$, or, substituting,

(4a) $\quad \bar{A}^s = \dfrac{v\Psi(\bar{K})}{p}.$

The equilibrium price of specie in terms of commodities that is established may or may not be a long-run equilibrium. Smith indicates that a mechanism exists to allocate specie among the nations of the world so that the price in an individual nation is equated with the world parity price, $\bar{p}$. The domestic supply of specie changes if $(p - \bar{p}) \neq 0$. Specifically,

(5) $\quad \Delta A^s = \gamma(p - \bar{p}).$

A favorable balance of payments occurs when $(p - \bar{p}) > 0$, and an unfavorable balance occurs when $(p - \bar{p}) < 0$. Short-run equilibrium exists in the individual nation if $A^s = A^d$, but long-run equilibrium requires $(p - \bar{p}) = 0$. Smith's message here, of course, is that money doesn't matter and certainly should not be an object of policy concern for the statesman.

Consider Smith's argument in graphic terms: Figure 4–1 depicts the specie market for an individual nation. The quantity of specie is measured on the horizontal axis and the price of specie in terms of commodities is measured on the vertical axis. The world price for specie in terms of commodities is determined at that level at which the supply of specie (= the world's stock of specie) is equated to the demand for specie (= some proportion of the world's supply of commodities). The world price of specie is viewed by the individual nation as a perfectly elastic price line (shown as the broken line, $\bar{p}$) in Figure 4–1. The individual nation's supply of specie is given and is shown as a vertical line A^s; the nation's demand for specie is drawn for a given full-employment output of commodities and is shown in Figure 4–1 as the line A^d which forms a rectangular hyperbola.

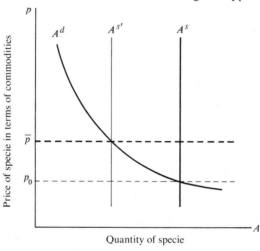

FIGURE 4–1

The price of specie within the individual country can diverge from the world price for only a short time. For example, if the short-run price of specie within the individual nation was equal to p_o in Figure 4–1, the low domestic price of specie relative to the world parity price would lead to an export of specie. The export of specie would, in turn, shift the specie supply curve leftward to $A^{s'}$, thereby raising the domestic price of specie in terms of commodities to the world parity level.

Smith emphasized, in effect, that the demand schedule drawn in Figure 4–1 is quite independent of the supply schedule. As has been noted, the demand for specie is some function of the economy's total output. Since output in Smith's economy is a function of capital stock, we may picture a family of demand-for-specie schedules, one for each level of capital stock.

As capital stock (and output) increases, we move from a lower to a higher demand schedule. The new higher demand schedule causes an initial increase in the domestic commodity price of specie above its world parity level and specie then flows into the country. The model thus reveals the basis for Smith's contention that the money supply adjusts passively to the needs of trade, a point ably summarized in the following passage:

> The quantity of money ... must in every country naturally increase as the value of the annual produce increases. The value of the consumable goods annually circulated within the society being greater, will require a greater quantity of money to circulate them. A part of the increased produce, therefore, will naturally be employed in purchasing, wherever it is to be had, the additional quantity of gold and silver necessary for circulating the rest. The increase of those metals will in this case be the effect, not the cause, of the public prosperity.[10]

Because of the ready adjustments in the money supply, Smith emphasized that a growing economy faces no shortage of circulating medium.[11] Economic growth thus provides the means for supplying the country with specie.[12]

III. "Money Doesn't Matter": Say's Law of Market Exchange

Say's Law of Markets met the design requirements of the basic classical model admirably well. As a theoretical explanation of commodity exchange, Say's Law describes the activity of the exchange period as a hitchless process that intervenes between two production periods. It may be seen as a logical extension of the period-analytic structure of the basic

---

10. Smith, *op. cit.*, pp. 323–24.

11. As long as the "balance of consumption" is favorable—that is, as long as savings is positive and capital is accumulating—growth will continue to take place, even in the face of a trade deficit. Smith asserts: "The balance of produce and consumption may be constantly in favour of a nation, though what is called the balance of trade be generally against it" (*ibid.*, p. 464). Smith's monetary model makes no provision for such a situation of economic growth accompanied by a loss of specie, and it is perhaps for this reason that Smith chooses to mention this anomalous case only in passing without attempting any analysis.

12. Something of a complication arises when the money supply includes bank notes. Smith indicated that a properly managed paper money is necessarily convertible at parity for specie (cf. *ibid.*, p. 308). So defined, bank notes serve equally as well as specie in meeting the economy's demand for circulating medium (cf. *ibid.*, p. 405). This argument has interesting implications for Smith's specie-flow model. With the money supply consisting of (1) specie and (2) convertible bank notes, an excess domestic demand for money could be met by an increase in bank notes instead of an influx of specie. Accordingly, specie would not cross

classical model. With classical economists opting for the simplifying assumption of a uniform duration of production activity in all industries, all commodities are placed on the market at the same time. This simultaneous completion of production in all commodity lines means that the total output is placed on the market at the same instant. From this point it was but a short step for James Mill to argue that "the production of commodities creates and is the one universal cause which creates a market for the commodities produced."[13] J. B. Say's elaborated statement of his Law of Markets[14] carries the same basic theme. Aggregate supply and aggregate demand are interdependent. Say argued that the commodities supplied to the market generate their own demand; though goods are exchanged for money, money serves strictly as a medium of exchange and does not affect the real level of aggregate demand. In all, money doesn't matter in Say's theory of aggregate demand. Say's method of analysis emphasizes the intermediary function of money: goods are supplied to the market and a money revenue is received that is then spent to purchase other goods. In essence, commodities are traded for commodities. One-half of the commodities placed on the market buys the other half. J. S. Mill

---

international borders when excess demand for money occurred. Bank-note issue would, in effect, prevent the commodity price of specie from rising and thereby would impede the operation of the price-specie-flow mechanism. This implied qualification is applicable only in a system featuring paper money. In a specie-standard system without bank notes, Smith's price-specie-flow mechanism operates in the classical manner.

On the question of bank-note issue, Smith offers the rule of thumb that a banking system composed of many banks and directed by sound principles would maintain the convertibility of bank notes at all times (cf. *ibid.*, p. 313). This "convertibility criterion" could thus only determine the *maximum* proportion of the total money supply that could be accounted for by bank notes. It defines the upward limit on the issue of bank notes and guarantees (1) that specie will not be completely displaced by bank notes and (2) that bank notes will continue to exchange at par value. Once the maximum extension of bank notes is attained, the occurrence of an (exogenously induced) adverse balance of payments brought about by a poor harvest would force the economy to behave as if its money supply consisted entirely of specie. The price of specie in terms of commodities would fall; specie would then be exported and the domestic supply of specie reduced. In addition, because the maximum extension of bank notes is proportional to domestic specie holdings, the export of specie would mean that bank notes would be reduced by some multiple of the exported specie. The presence of bank notes in the monetary system would, in this case, have the effect of requiring smaller international movements of specie to bring about the necessary domestic price adjustment within a country. Because the convertibility criterion for bank-note issue defines the maximum quantity of bank notes that can be issued and still maintain convertibility, it assures that bank notes will be passive in their impact on the balance of payments.

13. James Mill, *Commerce Defended* (1808), New York: Augustus M. Kelley, 1965, p. 81.

14. Jean-Baptiste Say, *A Treatise on Political Economy* (1803), New York: Augustus M. Kelley, 1964. Book I, Chapter XV.

concisely summarized Say's principle in pointing out that the means of payment for commodities "... is simply commodities. Each person's means for paying for the productions of other people consists of those which he himself possesses. All sellers are inevitably and *ex vi termini* buyers."[15] Say's insistence on the transactions function of money— money's exclusive use as a medium of exchange—is the result of, as well as contributing cause to, classical theory's rejection of the money supply as a key analytical variable.

Exposition of the formal relationships underlying Say's Law of Markets requires that market demand schedules be specified for each commodity in the form $Q_i^d = f_i(p_i)$, where Q_i^d is the quantity of the ith commodity demanded, p_i is money price, $i = 1 \cdots n$, and $f_i' < 0$. With the (implicit) classical requirement that demand functions be homogeneous of degree zero in money prices, commodity demand may be defined as a function of relative price: $Q_i^d = \phi_i(\lambda_i)$, where λ_i is the relative price $(= p_i/p_n = p_1/p_n, \cdots p_{n-1}/p_n, 1)$, and $p_i = p_n\lambda_i$. Homogeneity means here that all prices move *pari passu*—if one price doubles, all prices double. It implies an across-the-board shift in demand schedules so that if all money prices are doubled the quantities demanded do not change. For convenience, the demand equations may be expressed

(1) $Q_i^d = f_i(p_n\lambda_i)$.

The quantity of each commodity supplied to the market is given at the outset of the exchange period, $Q_i^s = \bar{Q}_i^s$, and equilibrium in each market prevails when

(2) $Q_i^d = Q_i^s$.

In the aggregate picture, the stock of commodities supplied to the market creates a flow demand for money,

(3) $p_n \sum_1^n \lambda_i Q_i^s = G^d$.

Simultaneously as sales of these commodities generate a flow of money revenue, G^s, the receipts are immediately spent and a demand for commodities created:

---

15. John Stuart Mill, *Principles of Political Economy* (1848; Ashley ed., 1909). New York: Augustus M. Kelley, 1969, pp. 557–58.

(4) $\quad p_n \sum_1^n \lambda_i Q_i^d = G^s.$

Taken together, equations (3) and (4) represent the exchange process between commodities, with money serving as the intermediating link. Exchange involves two steps: (1) moving from one set of commodities into money and (2) moving out of money into another set of commodities. Say's assertion that "money has no other function than to buy with" may be interpreted to mean that no one seeks to augment his cash holdings, i.e.,

(5) $\quad G^d \equiv G^s.$

This last equation has been labeled in the recent literature as "Say's identity." It necessarily implies that the given quantity of commodities supplied to the market is always fully cleared, having, in effect, generated its own demand:

(6) $\quad p_n \sum_1^n \lambda_i Q_i^s \equiv p_n \sum_1^n \lambda_i Q_i^d.$

Survey of the above system of equations reveals that there are $2n + 3$ equations (equations (1)–(5)), but only $2n + 2$ unknowns (Q_i^d, p_i, G^d, G^s). One step to remedy this over-determined system is found in the fact that the market relationship of one commodity is implied by equation (6). That is to say, if $n - 1$ commodities are cleared in the market, the nth commodity must also be cleared:

(7) $\quad p_n \sum_1^{n-1} \lambda_i Q_i^s + p_n Q_n^s \equiv p_n \sum_1^{n-1} \lambda_i Q_i^d + p_n Q_n^d.$

Thus, equation (6) implies

(8) $\quad p_n \sum_1^{n-1} \lambda_i Q_i^s \equiv p_n \sum_1^{n-1} \lambda_i Q_i^d.$

In brief, then, the one equation for the nth commodity, $p_n Q_n^s = p_n Q_n^d$, may be deleted from the count of independent relationships in the system. At this stage in the exposition, therefore, the number of unknowns and equations are identical ($= 2n + 2$).

The system, as presented so far, deals with money as a flow variable. G^s and G^d are the total flow of money expenditures and revenue over the exchange period. Neither the stock of money nor the relationship between the stock of money and the total flow of money expenditures is specified.

As a consequence, no constraint is placed on the price level and the general level of prices is left undetermined. Given equilibrium in relative prices, any general price level may prevail. In general, introduction of a money stock restraint on the system makes the absolute level of prices determinate. The particular task is accomplished by the equation of exchange, which specifies a linear relationship between p_n and the money stock. Using the Cambridge version of the equation of exchange we have

$$(9) \quad kp_n \sum_1^n \lambda_i Q_i^s = M^d,$$

where k is the reciprocal of the velocity of the money stock, p_n is the money price of the nth commodity, and M^d is the stock demand for money. With the money supply given, $M^s = \bar{M}^s$, equality in the supply of and demand for the stock of money is implied by equation (5). By definition, if the flow demand is identical with the flow supply of money, the stock demand must equal the stock supply of money, that is, if $G^d \equiv G^s$, then $M^d = M^s$. Accordingly, equilibrium in the money market exists when

$$(10) \quad E = M^d - M^s = kp_n \sum_1^n \lambda_i \bar{Q}_i^s - \bar{M}^s = 0,$$

where E is the excess demand for money. The system is now determinate: there are $2n + 3$ unknowns (Q_i^d, p_i, G^d, G^s, M^d) and $2n + 3$ equations (equations (1)–(5)—from which one relation is deleted à la equation (7)— and (9)). If the given stock of money, $\bar{M}^s$, were to increase, an excess supply of money ($E < 0$) would appear. Since $\bar{Q}^s$ and k are constant, the equilibrating process is worked out through an increase in p_n. In this way an increase in the money supply above a previously established equilibrium level leads to an increase in the general price level as the means to restore equilibrium. Inasmuch as demand functions are homogeneous of zero degree, the increase in p_n, which restores equilibrium in the money market, is also associated with a simultaneous and proportional increase in all commodity prices in terms of money.

In conclusion it is appropriate to call attention once again to the unimportance of the stock of money in classical analysis. For the most part this outcome is dictated by classical period analysis which specified a given supply of goods for the exchange period and opened no possibility whereby money demand for commodities could affect anything other than the price level. The equation of exchange that is employed in equation (10) illustrates the equilibrating process whereby a determinate general price level is established for the system. In the process, however, it lends further support to the notion that the money supply was of no real consequence for the classical model. The money supply in classical analysis, like French nobles at Versailles, had a place at court and an opportunity to be seen— but no real power to exercise in the outcome of history.

IV. Overview

The monetary side of classical analysis, with its underlying theme that "money doesn't matter," was molded by two main forces: (1) the theory and rhetoric of the clash with mercantilist thought and (2) the formal structure of the basic classical model. In the formative years of classical thought the paradigmatic confrontation with mercantilist thought dominated the analysis of the role of money. During these early years one main task of theoretical argumentation was to shift the center of economic discourse from money to capital. The new economics required an effective means to refute the basic tenet of latter-day mercantilism that the money supply is central to an explication of how the economy functions. By combining the classical aggregate supply function with the equation of exchange, thereby forging the classical version of the quantity theory of money, classical economics synthesized the price-specie-flow doctrine that met this requirement admirably. Since classical theory specified aggregate supply to be a function of previously accumulated capital stock, changes in the money supply could affect only the price level. It was this conceptualization of money's role that broke the linchpin of mercantilist theory.

The money-supply variable was continued in a subservient position by the period-analytic format of classical theory which provided no opening through which the money supply could be introduced to influence the level of real activity. In the commodity market, the supply of goods was assumed to be on hand at the outset of the exchange period. Changes in the money supply could therefore only affect the general level of commodity prices. Similarly, in the production period, capital stock is previously accumulated and there is no possibility that changes in the money supply can change capital stock and thereby influence the level of output. The one acknowledged exception to this last rule is the special case of "forced saving." This forced frugality occurs when monetary inflation is accompanied by a greater increase in the prices of wage goods than in the money wage rate. The net effect is an increase in capital stock brought about by a shift in the composition of capital stock (circulating capital is reduced and fixed capital is increased). But overall the effect was assigned little importance. Changes in the velocity of money were treated in the same way as changes in the money supply. Attempts to demonstrate that commodity gluts can arise from an increase in the desire to hold money failed as theoretical ventures because such arguments required a simultaneous circular-flow format which classical theory did not provide. The period-analytic format of classical theory forced the use of static equilibrium analysis and the acceptance of classical aggregate demand theory. Invariably, would-be monetary theorists failed the signal task of restructuring the basic classical model. They recognized the *empirical* relevance of money but failed at the theoretical task of formulating an aggregate demand theory in which the monetary side of the economy was demonstrably relevant for economic analysis.

APPENDIX TO CHAPTER FOUR
The Thornton-Wicksell Theory
of Credit Creation

The theory of credit creation, specifically the theory of bank-note issue, received serious but not extensive attention during the classical era. The leading contributions to the theory of credit creation were made by Henry Thornton and Knut Wicksell. Though publishing almost a century apart (1802 and 1898) both present the same underlying theme that credit creation is part of the maximizing behavior of individuals. The mode of explication of each is characteristically classical and similarities with the theories of classical capital accumulation and allocation are easily discernible. The theory of credit creation developed more as a response to external conditions—the British bullionist controversy in the case of Thornton and the bimetalism debates in the case of Wicksell—and is not (except in method of approach) part of the analytical unfolding of classical economics. Money and credit had to be explained "because they were there," but the explanation was peripheral to the workings of the basic classical model.

I. Thornton's Pioneer Insight

Henry Thornton's *Enquiry into the Nature and Effects of the Paper Credit of Great Britain*[1] is a many-sided study of British monetary institutions, processes, and problems at the outset of the nineteenth century. His coverage of the essential aspects of the theory of credit creation is brief and concise. According to Thornton's argument, the supply of loanable funds is provided either through individual savings or through credit creation by the banks. Whether funds are actually borrowed from the banks depends on the level of the bank rate of interest relative to the prevailing market rate of interest. The market or "mercantile" rate of interest in Thornton's analysis is analogous in function to the "natural price," "subsistence wage," or "normal profit" concepts used elsewhere in classical theory. That is to say, the market rate of interest serves as a conceptual bench mark with which to compare the bank rate of interest. If the market rate and the bank rate of interest are equal, no net credit creation takes place; on the other hand, if the bank rate is lower than the market rate, credit expansion occurs. The crux of Thornton's approach is stated in the following paragraph:

> In order to ascertain how far the desire of obtaining loans at the bank may be expected at any time to be carried, we must enquire into the subject of the quantum of profit likely to be derived from borrowing there under the existing circumstances. This is to be judged of by considering two points: the amount, first of interest to be paid on the sum borrowed; and, secondly, of the mercantile or other gain to be obtained by the employment of the borrowed capital. The gain which can be acquired by the means of commerce is commonly the highest which can be had; and it also regulates, in a great measure, the rate in all other cases. We may, therefore, consider this question as turning principally on a comparison of the rate of interest taken at the bank with the current rate of mercantile profit.[2]

Some years later, David Ricardo summarized the position with an additional measure of precision:

1. Henry Thornton, *An Enquiry into the Nature and Effects of Paper Credit in Great Britain* (1802), (edited with an introduction by F. A. Hayek), New York: Augustus M. Kelley, 1962. It should be noted that there is an intriguing parallel between Thornton's 1802 study and that by Pehr Niclas Christiernin, a Swedish academic economist, who wrote his major work in 1761. See Robert V. Eagly's "The Swedish and English Bullionist Controversies," contained in *Events, Ideology, and Economic Theory* (R. V. Eagly, editor), Detroit: Wayne State University Press, 1968, pp. 13–31.

2. Thornton, *op. cit.*, pp. 253–54.

The applications to the bank for money, then, depend on the comparison between the rate of profits that may be made by the employment of it and the rate at which they are willing to lend it. If they charge less than the market rate of interest, there is no amount of money which they might not lend; if they charge more than that rate none but spendthrifts and prodigals would be found to borrow of them. We accordingly find that when the market rate of interest exceeds the rate of 5 per cent. at which the Bank uniformly lend, the discount office is beseiged with applicants for money; and, on the contrary, when the market rate is even temporarily under 5 per cent., the clerks of that office have no employment.[3]

II. Wicksellian Model of Credit Creation

Credit creation was the important question to which Knut Wicksell addressed himself at the end of the nineteenth century.[4] In the Wicksellian monetary model the interest rate is the pivotal variable. Briefly described, Wicksell's model stipulates that changes in the economy's money stock originate from a disparity between the bank rate of interest and the normal rate of interest. A more detailed exposition of the salient elements of the Wicksellian monetary model incorporates the following symbols:

$\bar{y}$ = output (is given once the economy's total capital stock is specified)

p = the general price level

Y = money value of national output ($= py$)

S = net savings (net change in time deposits)

I = net demand for credit (demand for new loans less repayment of old loans)

M^d = money stock demanded

M^s = money stock supplied (demand deposits)[5]

E_b = the bank rate of interest (loan rate and deposit rate)

E_n = the normal rate of interest

$t, t-1$ = time subscripts.

The demand for money is generated by transactions as specified in the equation of exchange:

3. David Ricardo, *The Principles of Political Economy and Taxation* (1817), London: J. M. Dent & Sons, Ltd., 1955, p. 246.
4. Knut Wicksell, *Interest and Prices* (1898), (translated by R. F. Kahn), London, 1936.
5. This exposition assumes the existence of a Wicksellian pure credit system in which the money supply consists of demand deposits. Cf. *ibid.*, pp. 68ff.

(1) $\quad M_t^d = kY_t$.

On the supply side, two determinants are specified. First, the supply of money available in period t is, in part, inherited from the preceding period, $t - 1$. And second, the change in the money supply during period t is defined as the difference between the net demand for credit from the commercial-central bank and the net savings that occurs during the same period. We specify that the commercial-central bank extends credit to all who apply for loans and are willing to pay the bank rate of interest, and that all individual savings take the form of time deposits in the economy's central bank which also serves as the sole commercial bank of the system. Time deposits are not part of the money supply. There is no market for stocks or bonds in the model and the central bank assumes the role of financial intermediary in the system. The total supply of money for period t then becomes:

(2) $\quad M_t^s = M_{t-1}^s + (I_t - S_t)$,

where $(I_t - S_t)$ is the net credit creation by the bank. In equilibrium, the demand for money in period t is equal to the supply of money in period t:

(3) $\quad M_t^s = M_t^d$,

or, substituting (1) and (2) into (3),

(4) $\quad M_{t-1}^s + (I_t - S_t) = kY_t$.

Equation (4) implies that the money supply and the price level will change in the same direction as the sign of the difference $(I_t - S_t)$. That is,

(5) $\quad M_t^s - M_{t-1}^s = I_t - S_t$, and

(6) $\quad p_t - p_{t-1} = (1/k\bar{y})(I_t - S_t)$.

Both savings and the demand for credit are functions of the bank rate of interest. For the sake of simplicity, the assumption is made that the bank pays the same interest rate on savings deposits as it receives from loans.[6] These functions are:

(7) $\quad S_t = \alpha_1 + \beta_1 E_{b_t}$, and

(8) $\quad I_t = \alpha_2 - \beta_2 E_{b_t}$,

where E_{b_t} is set by the bank.

---

6. *Ibid.*, p. 140.

Substitution of (7) and (8) into equations (5) and (6) reveals the key role played by the bank rate of interest in the Wicksellian system:

(5a) $M_t^s - M_{t-1}^s = [(\alpha_2 - \alpha_1) - E_{b_t}(\beta_1 + \beta_2)]$, and

(6a) $p_t - p_{t-1} = (1/k\bar{y})[(\alpha_2 - \alpha_1) - E_{d_t}(\beta_1 + \beta_2)]$.

The independent variable in equations (5a) and (6a) is the bank rate of interest, E_b. There exists but one value for E_{b_t} at which net savings is equated to the net demand for credit for the period. This condition provides a continuing equilibrium by ensuring that $M_{t-1}^s = M_t^s$. If we designate this equilibrium interest rate as the "normal" rate of interest,[7] E_n, the pivotal role of the bank rate of interest can be readily demonstrated. Letting $\beta_3 = (\beta_1 + \beta_2)$, the change in the money supply is described as

(9) $\Delta M_t^s = \beta_3(E_n - E_{b_t})$;

and the change in the price level is expressed as

(10) $\Delta p_t = (1/k\bar{y})[\beta_3(E_n - E_{b_t})]$.

The implications of the Wicksellian model are summarized in Table 4–A1.

TABLE 4–A1

CONDITION	INTEREST RATE RELATION	CHANGE IN MONEY SUPPLY (credit creation)	CHANGE IN PRICE LEVEL
Equilibrium	$E_{b_t} = E_n$	$\Delta M_t^s = 0$	$\Delta p_t = 0$
Inflation	$E_{b_t} < E_n$	$\Delta M_t^s > 0$	$\Delta p_t > 0$
Deflation	$E_{b_t} > E_n$	$\Delta M_t^s < 0$	$\Delta p_t < 0$

Maintenance of a constant price level—a Wicksellian policy norm—becomes a matter of maintaining the proper interest rate through central bank action. If $E_{b_t} \neq E_n$, the price level and the money supply would

---

7. *Ibid.*, p. 120: "At any moment and in every economic situation there is a certain level of the average rate of interest which is such that the general level of prices has no tendency to move either upwards or downwards. This we call the *normal* rate of interest."

continue to change, i.e., continuously increasing or decreasing as the case may be. This disequilibrium process—Wicksell's cumulative process—continues until the bank rate of interest is again equated with the normal rate of interest. When equilibrium is re-established, the price level will come to rest at a higher (or lower) level. The new equilibrium price level will be permanent until a divergence between E_b and E_n reappears. In brief, banking policy should follow these main lines in regulating credit creation:

> So long as prices remain unaltered the banks' rate of interest is to remain un-altered. If prices rise, the rate of interest is to be raised; and if prices fall, the rate of interest is to be lowered; and the rate of interest is henceforth to be maintained at its new level until a further movement of prices calls for a further change in one direction or another.[8]

In this way Wicksell argued that while changes in the money supply were associated with changes in the general price level, the actual causal relationship was much more complex. Wicksell's monetary model stressed the key role of the bank rate of interest and demonstrated that changes in the price level and the money supply are themselves functions of a third variable, namely, the difference between the bank rate and the normal rate of interest.

---

8. *Ibid.*, p. 189.

Cyclical downturns in British business activity in the early nineteenth century gave stimulus to controversy over the nature and origin of commodity "gluts." The accompanying discussion raised issues that exposed aggregate demand theory to be a comparatively neglected side of classical economic theory. To fill the gap in classical analysis, contributions by J. B. Say[1] and J. Mill[2], under the latter-day rubric of Say's Law, provided a theoretical explanation of aggregate market demand that fit in admirably well with the developing edifice of classical economic theory. The success of Say's Law, despite its inconsistency with the observed recession phenomena of unemployment and unwanted inventories, is one measure of the dominance of classical analysis at the outset of the nineteenth century. To be effective, a critique of Say's Law had to meet two major criteria: (1) it had to be consistent with classical economics' theory of production; and (2) it had to provide a coherent alternative theory of aggregate demand—for as has been observed in the history of science, theories are displaced by other theories rather than destroyed by anomalous empirical findings. Writers who offered explanations of commodity gluts stressed observation rather than theoretical analysis and too often attempted to work outside the post-Quesnaysian analytical tradition. By attempting too much they were exceedingly vulnerable to refutation.

The critique of Say's Law that was conveyed in the aggregative model

1. Jean-Baptiste Say, *A Treatise on Political Economy* (1803), 1st American ed. (4th French edition), 1821, New York: Augustus M. Kelley, 1964, Chapter XV, pp. 132–40.
2. James Mill, *Commerce Defended*, 1808.

offered by T. R. Malthus was structured within the framework of classical theory. It offered a modification, not an overthrow, of the analytics of classical economics. It was a main-line classical model that attempted to account for commodity gluts and unemployed labor in terms of its own aggregate demand theory. Malthus approached the problem by adding an additional sector (the service sector) to the one-sector classical model. The two-sector approach permitted Malthus to define aggregate demand to be dependent upon the reciprocal demands between the two sectors. The model emphasized the delicate balance required to keep both commodity and labor markets cleared. The challenge to Say's Law set down by T.R. Malthus raised an important issue concerning whether consumption and investment demand would clear the commodity market. Though the theoretical construction he suggested failed to gain formal acceptance, classical theory eventually responded to the theoretical question raised by the Malthusian aggregative model by incorporating a mechanism, namely, the loanable funds theory, that explained away the troubling quandary exposed by Malthus.

I. Say's Law and the Composition of Demand

As has been already detailed, the basic classical model demonstrated how those commodities that make up total capital stock are used for the production of more commodities and how the period-analytic format of classical analysis dichotomized the classical economy and effectively insulated production and exchange from one another. While classical economists indicated an awareness that production periods differ in length in different industries, they generalized as if there was a uniform gestation period in all industries. This served as a highly useful heuristic device. It gave basis to the supposition of the simultaneous marketing of the system's total commodity output and was the starting point for Say's Law of market exchange which was an extension from this basic format. With all commodities placed on the market at the outset of the exchange period, it was but a short analytical step to argue that supply creates its own demand.

It is important to stress that Say's Law was not the heartland of classical theory. It was, so to speak, merely a border outpost which main-line classical economists defended in order to keep competing "barbarian" theories from gaining ground and from attempting possible forays against the real heartland of classical theory in which capital was supreme, capitalists held sway, accumulation was praised, and production of commodities was the dominant religion.

That reciprocal demands constituted the basis for commodity market transactions is a fundamental principle recognized in the economic literature well before J. B. Say discussed the point. Say's approach was novel inasmuch as he dealt with commodity exchange on a disaggregative level. Transactors in the market were an undifferentiated group of capitalists whose only identifiable characteristic was a motivation to exchange goods which they had produced for other goods. The exact composition of marketed output was only an indirect concern of the exchange process which was resolved via the inter-industry allocation of capital. In classical theory the competitive norm specified a uniform profit rate over the different industries. Were the uniform profit rate norm not realized, capital would be reallocated among industries, thereby changing the composition of output. Any change in the pattern of demand from one exchange period to the next would influence the rate of profit in different industries, and subsequently influence the composition of output. Above all, the composition of output was seen to have no connection with the level of aggregate demand.

It is in regard to this point concerning the composition of output that T. R. Malthus attacked—and rejected—Say's doctrine. Malthus insisted that the specific composition of aggregate demand was of crucial importance and he argued that unless aggregate demand were properly "balanced," total output would not be cleared in the market in the way indicated by Say's Law. He accused adherents of Say's doctrine to have

> ...considered commodities as if they were so many mathematical figures, or arithmetical characters, the relations of which were to be compared, instead of articles of consumption, which must of course be referred to the numbers and wants of the consumers.[3]

According to Malthus, there exists some optimum balance between goods destined for accumulation and goods destined for consumption. Equilibrium in the economy is a very delicate balancing act, and, according to Malthus's model, Say's doctrine overlooked the restrictive conditions that must be satisfied for equilibrium to be established.

---

3. Thomas Robert Malthus, *Principles of Political Economy* (1820), 2nd edition, New York: Augustus M. Kelley, 1951, pp. 316–17.

The crux of Malthus's critique of Say's Law is to be found in the model's implication that the profit rate does not operate to establish an optimum composition of output. This derives from the fact that the Malthusian model incorporates the service sector and adds services to the exchange process.[4] Since capital is employed only in the commodity sector the profit rate can affect only the composition of commodity output. Services are produced in exchange for revenue.[5] By definition no capital is employed in the service sector. Accordingly, there is no profit return and no possibility that the production of services could be regulated by the same sort of mechanism that was specified to keep the one-sector classical system moving smoothly over time. The Malthusian aggregative model thus puts a direct theoretical challenge to the standard classical system. With no mechanism present to control the composition of output, there was a distinct possibility that a "wrong" combination of output eventually would be produced. Malthus's formal model went well beyond this implication, and specified the conditions for equilibrium that emphasized the interdependence between two sets of goods (commodities and services) and two sets of transactors (the productive sector and the unproductive sector).

II. The Malthusian Aggregative Model

While other classical economists recognized a class of service-producing unproductive labor in their analysis, they did not consider it to have sufficient importance or relevance to the operation of the system to incorporate it into the basic classical model. By contrast, Malthus singled

---

4. *Ibid.,* pp. 315–16. "It has been thought by some very able writers, that although there may easily be a glut of particular commodities, there cannot possibly be a glut of commodities in general; because, according to their view of the subject, commodities being always exchanged for commodities, one half will furnish a market for the other half, and production being thus the sole source of demand, an excess in the supply of one article merely proves a deficiency in the supply of some other, and a general excess is impossible .... This doctrine, however, as generally applied, appears to me to be utterly unfounded .... It is by no means true, as a matter of fact, that commodities are always exchanged for commodities. An immense mass of commodities is exchanged directly, either for productive labour, or personal services: and it is quite obvious that this mass of commodities, compared with the labour with which it is to be exchanged, may fall in value from a glut just as any one commodity falls in value from an excess of supply, compared either with labour or money."

5. *Ibid.,* p. 408. "It is farther to be remarked, that all personal services paid voluntarily, whether of a menial or intellectual kind, are essentially distinct from the labour necessary to production. They are paid from revenue, not from capital."

out the class of unproductive labor for special attention and emphasized the interdependence between it and productive labor in an intersectoral reciprocal demand situation. To signal the great significance he attached to this line of inquiry, Malthus wrote:

> There can hardly be a more important inquiry in political economy than that which traces the effects of different proportions of productive labour, and personal services in society.[6]

Malthus's model divides the total work force into two main categories:[7] (1) productive labor, N_1 (which produces material objects that can transferred); and (2) unproductive labor, N_2 (which produces non-transferable services). The distinction between these two groups was typically made by classical economists, but Malthus was the only post-Quesnaysian who incorporated the distinction and elaborated upon the point in the analytics of his model. The total demand for labor of both categories is then:

(1) $\quad N^d = N_1^d + N_2^d.$

Because the core of the capitalist system is the production of commodities by means of commodities, production in the "productive" or commodity-producing sector of the economy is defined to be a function of the system's total capital stock.[8] Production requires that the given total capital stock

6. *Ibid.*, p. 42, fn.

7. *Ibid.*, p. 35. "Labour may then be distinguished into two kinds, productive labour, and personal services (unproductive labour), meaning by productive labour that labour which is so directly productive of material wealth as to be capable of estimation in the quantity or value of the object produced, which object is capable of being transferred without the presence of the producer; and meaning by personal services that kind of labour or industry, which however highly useful and important some of it may be, and however much it may conduce *indirectly* to the production and security of material wealth, does not realize itself on any object which can be valued and transferred without the presence of the person performing such service, and cannot therefore be made to enter into an estimate of national wealth."

8. *Ibid.*, pp. 36–38. "It is obvious ... that it is only the productive labour of Adam Smith, which can keep up, restore, or increase, the material capital of a country. It is also this kind of labour alone, that is, the labour which is realized in the production, or increased value of material objects, which requires a considerable amount of capital for its continued employment. ... It is true, that what is called capital, is sometimes employed in the maintenance of labour, which is not called productive. ... But at all events, the amount of it is too inconsiderable to be allowed to interfere with a classification in other respects correct, and in the highest degree useful. ... In speaking therefore, and treating of capital, it seems highly useful to have some term for the kind of labour which it generally employs, in contradistinction to the kind of labour which in general is employed directly by revenue, in order to explain the nature of productive labour, and its peculiar efficiency in causing the increase of wealth."

($\overline{K}$) be allocated to variable capital and fixed capital. Both laborers and machines are required and are demanded by the capitalists. But, by definition, only productive labor is demanded by capitalist producers:

(2) $N_1^d = \overline{K}/(w + \overline{p}/\alpha)$,

where w is the wage per worker, $\overline{p}$ is the given price per unit of machinery (fixed capital), and α is the labor-machine ratio. Net commodity output[9] in the economy (Z) can be described as a function of the number of productive laborers employed:

(3) $Z^s = aN_1^s$.

In the model this net disposable commodity income can be spent in two ways—(1) for increments to capital stock (i.e., net investment (I)) and (2) for the services of unproductive labor (i.e., consumption (C)). That portion of commodities which is not invested is exchanged for personal services produced by unproductive labor. The exchange constitutes a reciprocal demand relationship between the productive labor sector and the unproductive labor sector. The supply of commodities placed on this intersectoral market may be defined as some proportion of net commodity output, that is,

(4) $C^s = cZ^s$.

The quantity of commodities offered for personal services constitutes the wage bill for the unproductive laborers. The demand for unproductive labor is

(5) $N_2^d = C^s/w$.

With the size of the total work force, $N^s(= N_1^s + N_2^s)$, assumed historically determined, $N^s = \overline{N}^s$, equilibrium prevails in the labor market when

(6a) $\overline{N}^s = N^d$, or, substituting from equations (1)–(5),

(6b) $\overline{N}^s = [\overline{K}/(w + \overline{p}/\alpha)](1 + ca/w)$.

The Malthusian labor market, as expressed by equations (1)–(6), emphasizes the interdependency between productive and unproductive labor. The model embraces both the production period and the exchange

---

9. Net commodity output is here defined as the value of commodity output net of those expenditures necessary to replace depreciated fixed capital and replenish variable capital.

period and thereby creates a simultaneous system that is a significant departure from the period-analytic format of the basic classical model. Specifically, the model includes in a single labor market both productive labor (which is paid from capital and is employed during the production period) and unproductive labor (which is paid from revenue and is employed during the exchange period). In other words, the demand for productive labor originates in prior accumulated capital stock while the demand for unproductive labor originates in the current period's expenditure of current output for non-commodity producing services. In keeping with the main thrust of the Malthusian analysis, we may stipulate the simultaneity of production and exchange relationships; i.e., a single unified labor market. This means that it is the wage rate (w) which is the variable which equilibrates the labor market and establishes equilibrium in equation (6b). Equilibrium in the labor market is a convenient point of departure for examining the nature and origin of disequilibrium in the intersectoral market. It is to the intersectoral market that we now turn.

In the intersectoral exchange, a certain quantity (C^s) of commodities is supplied by productive labor, and a certain quantity of services, $X^s (= \beta N_2^s)$, is supplied by unproductive labor. Each supply is produced and placed on the market to demand the other. Thus, $C^s = X^d$, and $X^s = C^d$. Both markets are cleared when $C^s = C^d$ and $X^s = X^d$. Equilibrium in the intersectoral market implies that $caN_1(1 - \beta/w) = 0$.[10]

Let us assume that an equilibrium wage rate prevails, and thus that labor is fully employed. Attention may then be turned to the question as to whether the total commodity market is cleared. As has been noted, the total demand for commodities is equal to consumption demand plus investment demand. That is,

(7) $\quad Z^d = C^d + I^d.$

Consumption demand for commodities (C^d) is equal to the quantity of commodities supplied to the market for purchase of unproductive services ($= cZ^s = caN_1$). Investment demand in the Malthusian model would appear to be determined as a function of the profit rate,[11] but for purposes

---

10. Since $C^s = X^s$ in equilibrium, successive substitution from equations (3)–(5) yields $cZ^s = X^s$, $caN_1 = \beta N_2$, $caN_1 = \beta C^s/w$, $caN_1 = \beta caN_1/w$, or finally $caN_1(1 - \beta/w) = 0$.

11. Malthus's *passim* discussion of the determinants of investment suggests an investment function that is the same as generally specified by classical economists since Adam Smith. Investment is defined as a function of the profit rate relative to the capitalists' minimum acceptable profit rate; that is, $I^d = f(r - \bar{r})$, where r is the profit rate, $\bar{r}$ is the minimum profit rate acceptable to capitalists, $f' > 0$, and $I^d = 0$ when $(\dot{r} - \bar{r}) = 0$.

here let us assume that investment demand is given; that is, $I^d = \bar{I}^d$. The critical point is that capitalists may or may not select the "correct" level of expenditures to maintain equilibrium at all times. Equilibrium in the commodity market requires that

(8a) $Z^s = Z^d$. By substitution we have,

(8b) $aN_1(1 - c) = \bar{I}^d$.

In equation (8b), equilibrium in the intersectoral market requires the "proper" level of investment expenditures by capitalists. *Herein lies the core of Malthus's critique of Say's Law.* The Malthusian model challenged classical aggregate demand theory by calling attention to the fact that investment demand may or may not clear the commodity market. In effect the argument emphasizes that investment must have a unique value in each exchange period; moreover, the correct level of investment is not likely to be achieved at all times.[12] In terms of Say's model, the decision to add to capital stock is made after the commodity market is cleared. For Malthus, the decision to demand commodities for investment is made simultaneously with the exchange transactions. The main point in the Malthusian model, however, is the interpretation that the expenditure decisions for consumption and for investment are made by two different sets of individuals. Because there is no co-ordination in the decisions of these two groups, commodity gluts may occur from time to time.

A graphic overview of the system is provided in Figure 5–1. The length of the horizontal axis measures the given total labor force ($\bar{N}^s$); productive labor is measured from the left and unproductive labor is measured from the right. Net commodity output is drawn as a function of productive labor and appears as the Z line originating in the left-hand corner of the diagram. Similarly, output of services is drawn as a function of unproductive labor and is shown as the X line that originates in the right-hand corner of the diagram. Both Z and X are expressed in labor value units, and equal distances of Z measured on the left-hand vertical axis exchange for equal distances of X measured on the right-hand vertical axis. Given the economy's total capital stock and an equilibrium wage rate, the

---

12. The model indicates that investment demand must increase every time period. This can be shown by rewriting equation (8), substituting $\bar{K}/(w + \bar{p}/\alpha)$ for N_1 and thereby obtaining $I^d = a(1 - c)[\bar{K}/(w + \bar{p}/\alpha)]$. Starting from an initial equilibrium condition, continuing equilibrium over time would require that the rate of growth of capital, I/K, equal the expression $a(1 - c)/(w + \bar{p}/\alpha)$. Given the values of the parameters, capital stock must thus increase at a constant percentage rate.

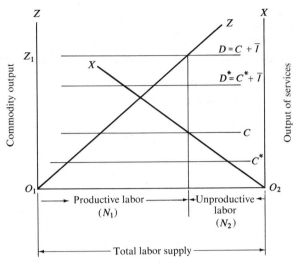

FIGURE 5–1

employment of productive labor is determined equal to O_1N_1, and the
employment of unproductive labor is O_2N_2. This level of employment is
associated with a net disposable commodity output equal to O_1Z_1
(measured on the left-hand vertical axis). Assumption of Say's Law for
commodities requires that the aggregate demand schedule for commodities, D, be drawn to intersect the Z line at this level of employment
(O_1N_1). General equilibrium in the model then is associated with unique
values of investment and consumption expenditures as well as a unique
division of the work force between productive and unproductive labor.
The D line is the horizontal summation of consumption and investment
demand ($= C^d + I^d$). The C line, which represents the reciprocal demand
between productive and unproductive labor, marks off the amounts of
commodities on the Z axis and services on the X axis which are exchanged.
In terms of the model, the stationary state exists when the C line, the Z
schedule, and the X schedule all intersect at the same point. With no net
investment there would be no growth. The interdependence of productive
and unproductive labor would then constitute the whole story of maintaining aggregate demand. The uniqueness of the composition of commodity demand and the strategic importance of the reciprocal exchange
between productive and unproductive labor are immediately evident in
this graphic presentation of the Malthusian system. Say's Law—the

principle that supply generates its own demand—is not sufficient in itself to explain (or satisfy) the condition of equilibrium in Malthus's model. It embodies no mechanism to assure the correct composition of demand.

The policy implications of the Malthusian model were centered upon the means to stimulate increases in consumption expenditures. Investment demand was not regarded to be a policy parameter. Increases in investment, by augmenting production capacity, would have a perverse effect upon commodity gluts. At best, any increase in investment would be a very short-run expedient. The basic problem would be only postponed— to emerge again later on. Accordingly, Malthus argued that policy measures must be taken to increase consumption. In all, Malthus evaluated four main categories of consumers with respect to their capacity to increase consumption expenditures. Capitalists, to begin with, could not be expected to enlarge their expenditures for luxury goods or for the services of unproductive labor because, Malthus held, "such consumption is not consistent with the actual habits of the generality of capitalists."[13] Wage-earners as a class were also irrelevant to a solution of the glut problem. According to Malthus, an increase in wages would reduce the supply of labor and reduce aggregate supply rather than increase aggregate demand.[14] In addition, an increase in wages would reduce the profit rate and discourage investment demand too violently.[15] Wage increases then were not the answer. The one large income class that could contribute

---

13. Malthus, *op. cit.*, p. 400.

14. *Ibid.*, p. 334. "It is the want of *necessaries* which mainly stimulates the labouring classes to produce luxuries; and were this stimulus removed or greatly weakened, so that the necessaries of life could be obtained with very little labour, instead of more time being devoted to the production of conveniences, there is every reason to think that less time would be so devoted."

15. *Ibid.*, pp. 404–5. "It has appeared then that, in the ordinary state of society, the master producers and capitalists, though they may have the power, have not the will, to consume in the shape of revenue to the necessary extent. And with regard to their workmen, it must be allowed that, if they possessed the will, they have not the power. It is indeed most important to observe that no power of consumption on the part of the labouring classes can ever, according to the common motives which influence mankind, alone furnish an encouragement to the employment of capital. No one will ever employ capital merely for the sake of the demand occasioned by those who work for him.... But as a great increase of consumption among the working classes must greatly increase the cost of production, it must lower profits, and diminish or destroy the motive to accumulate, before agriculture, manufactures, and commerce have reached any considerable degree of prosperity. If each labourer were actually to consume double the quantity of corn which he does at present, such a demand, instead of giving a stimulus to wealth, would unquestionably throw a great quantity of land out of cultivation, and greatly diminish both internal and external commerce."

to augmenting consumption expenditures was the landlords.[16] Malthus called upon this group to increase its expenditures for non-productive labor and luxuries—from a sense of national duty if not of personal utility. In addition, Malthus recognized that government has the potential to play a very significant role as a non-productive consumer.[17] Taxation of net disposable commodity output provides government the commodity means to support non-productive labor (soldiers, sailors, judges, etc.). For example, in terms of Malthus's model, increases in the consumption expenditures of the landlords and the tax-financed government would serve to increase c, shifting the C^* and D^* schedules in Figure 5–1 upward to C and D. This means an increased amount of commodities placed on the intersectoral market and, in turn, an increase in the employment of unproductive labor. The glut or overproduction of commodities is thus eliminated by the increased consumption demand; i.e., increased demand for the services of unproductive labor.

III. Post-Malthusian Developments: The Loanable Funds Theory

Malthus's critique of Say's Law readily survived a rebuttal attempt by J. B. Say,[18] but it nevertheless failed to gain acceptance in main-line classical economic theory. In part no doubt, some lack of conciseness in Malthus's exposition lessened his influence. In addition, acceptance of his views was reduced by the belief that Malthus wished to de-emphasize capital accumulation—a position that was virtual heresy to many classical economists. But there were more important analytical reasons for the

---

16. *Ibid.,* p. 400. "There must therefore be a considerable class of persons who have both the will and power to consume more material wealth than they produce, or the mercantile classes could not continue profitably to produce so much more than they consume. In this class the landlords no doubt stand pre-eminent; but if they were not assisted by the great mass of individuals engaged in personal services, whom they maintain, their own consumption would of itself be insufficient to keep up the increase the value of the produce, and enable the increase of its quantity more than to counterbalance the fall of its price."

17. *Ibid.,* p. 409. "With regard to these latter classes [those which must be supported by taxation], such as statesmen, soldiers, sailors, and those who live upon the interest of a national debt, it cannot be denied that they contribute powerfully to distribution and demand; they frequently occasion a division of property more favourable to the progress of wealth than would otherwise have taken place; they ensure that effective consumption which is necessary to give the proper stimulus to production; and the desire to pay a tax, and yet enjoy the same means of gratification, must often operate to excite the exertions of industry quite as effectually as the desire to pay a lawyer or physician."

18. J. B. Say, *Letters to Mr. Malthus on Several Subjects of Political Economy and on the Cause of the Stagnation of Commerce* (1821), New York: Augustus M. Kelley, 1967.

failure of the Malthusian model. First, two-sector models were in general disfavor. They involved additional complexity that was itself unwelcomed. The multisectoral, demand-oriented models of the eighteenth century to which Malthus's model bore some parallel, especially the type model set forth by Sir James Steuart, had largely been pushed out of sight in the economics literature of the early nineteenth century. Single-sector, two-period analysis was the main-line classical approach. The simplicity of Say's Law was admirably suited to these structural characteristics of classical theory. Though Malthus's critique may have occasioned some concern, especially in view of the contemporary British recession, it did not disrupt the course of analytical development of classical economics. What took place, as we can see in retrospect, was a theoretical accommodation to the issues raised by Malthus.

Within the context of a single-sector model, main-line classical theory did come to grips with the important Malthusian question of how net income is divided between consumption expenditures and investment expenditures.[19] Malthus's critique of Say's Law made the point that classical theory had not conceptualized a mechanism designed to perform this particular task. The theoretical mechanism that was designed to meet this criticism is the loanable funds theory. Within the framework of the one-sector basic classical model, the loanable funds market served as the mechanism to divide commodity output between investment and consumption. On the one side of the market, individuals decided whether to save or to consume by relating the interest rate to their willingness to abstain from consumption.[20] By definition income that is not consumed is

---

19. John Stuart Mill, *Principles of Political Economy* (1848; Ashley ed., 1909), New York: Augustus M. Kelley, 1969, pp. 163–64: "The fund from which saving can be made, is the surplus of the produce of labour, after supplying the necessaries of life to all concerned in the production: including those employed in replacing the materials, and keeping the fixed capital in repair. More than this surplus cannot be saved under any circumstances. As much as this, though it is never saved, always might be. This surplus is the fund from which the enjoyments, as distinguished from the necessaries, of the producers are provided; it is the fund from which all additions are made to capital. It is the real net produce of the country.... The amount of this fund, this net produce ... is one of the elements that determine the amount of saving. A part of the motive to saving consists in the prospect of deriving an income from savings.... The greater the profit that can be made from capital, the stronger is the motive to its accumulation."

20. *Ibid.*, pp. 405–6: "This [the equivalent a solvent person would be willing to pay for the loan of capital], which as everybody knows is called interest, is all that a person is enabled to get by merely abstaining from the immediate consumption of his capital and allowing it to be used for productive purposes by others. The remuneration which is obtained in any country for mere abstinence, is measured by the current rate of interest on the best security; such security as precludes any appreciable chance of losing the principal."

saved. Simply stated, savings was specified to be a positive function and (by implication) consumption a negative function of the interest rate. Any given interest rate locates a unique point on this function and is then associated with a unique division of income between the two alternative uses.

An extension of this approach to the problem of dividing net output between investment and consumption was provided by the loanable funds mechanism. The savings-consumption function described in the preceding paragraph is the supply side of the loanable funds market. The demand side of the market is based (1) largely on the demand for investment goods that is stimulated by the prospective profit rate and (2) partly on the demand for consumption loans by the government and private individuals in the community. Each of these demand elements may be defined as negative functions of the interest rate. Combined, these two market functions determine an equilibrium rate of interest and directly provide the apparatus by which the net product is demonstrably divided between non-productive and productive expenditures. The loanable funds market is thus seen to employ the joint principles of productivity and thrift for linking together the commodity sector and the service sector. Since investment expenditures are limited to the level which is warranted by profits they do not and cannot become "excessive"; and since what is not saved is necessarily consumed, insufficiency of aggregate demand cannot arise. The impact of the argument was to remove the very basis to Malthus's critique against Say's Law. For a detailed discussion of the loanable funds theory see Chapter 3, section VI.

The loanable funds theory provided an effective counter-argument against the Malthusian claim that commodity gluts may arise because investment demand and consumption demand are determined independently. What post-Malthusian classical economists accomplished by way of developing the loanable funds theory was to provide theoretical support for Say's Law by showing that net output was either consumed or invested. Specifically, they eliminated the main basis for Malthus's critique of Say's Law. And, in the process, Malthus's aggregative model was shunted off the main track of classical economic theory.

Business Fluctuations in the Classical System 6
Karl Marx's Real Endogenous Cycle

Classical economists were not unaware of the empirical reality of fluctuations in the level of economic activity. The problem they encountered in dealing with the business cycle was not in acknowledging the facts of economic life but in conceptualizing business fluctuations within a formal theory. It was not until the main principles of the basic classical model had been set down that classical economics was addressed to the task of explaining the business cycle. In large measure, analysis of the cycle in classical economics was delayed because of the emphasis placed on real phenomena and the considerable complexity of formulating a real theory of the business cycle. Attempts to explain the business cycle in terms of a monetary-linked breakdown in the exchange process invariably ran counter to the dominant classical view that the money supply was an entirely passive variable in the system. Unless they were based on a fully developed alternative theory of money there was no chance that arguments asserting the non-operation of Say's Law could gain wide acceptance. To be consistent with the rest of classical analysis, a theory of the business cycle had to be cast in terms of real phenomena.

The breakthrough in analyzing the cyclical dynamics of the classical model was made by Karl Marx. Because of his concern with "the laws of capitalist motion," Marx identified the business cycle and the exploitation of labor as the hallmarks of the capitalist system. He visualized capitalism to be a highly dynamic machine which was kept constantly in motion by the continual and interacting pressures of capital accumulation, technological change, and the reserve army of unemployed. Marx's new departure as a classical theorist was to dynamize the basic classical model. Specifically, Marx introduced technological change. This innovative step, in making technological change an endogenous part of the classical model, provided the basis for a classical theory of the business cycle.

This chapter presents a model of Marx's macro economy that permits analysis of both static equilibrium conditions as well as the properties of the dynamic cyclical pattern of the system. In its static version, the model gives an equilibrium solution that determines the unemployment level, the rate of exploitation, and the profit rate. When dynamized, the model provides the basis for analyzing the determinants of the Marxist business cycle. It demonstrates a self-generating endogenous cycle in which the unemployment rate increases from trough to trough in successive cycles. The model thus formulates Marxist analysis in a manner that permits a concise overview of the working of the system. Moreover, since the endogenous cycle is shown to exist under the classical assumption that the commodity market is always cleared, the model reveals how Marx's theory of the labor market and conceptualization of technological change provided the modification of classical economic theory that was necessary to provide a theoretical explanation of cyclical business fluctuations.

I. Some Preliminary Considerations

As a classical economist, Marx regarded capital to be not only the single most important variable in the economic system but the most significant unifying analytical construct for economic theory as well. Capital was seen to be a fund of resources composed of machinery, raw materials, and subsistence for the work force. The capitalists in the system allocated the economy's total capital stock between these three categories, taking into account existing technological coefficients and market prices. Profit maximization governed the behavior of the capitalists to ensure that capital was optimally allocated between industries and between sectors. While other classical economists emphasized the smooth functioning of the economy, Marx insisted that it moved by fits and starts. The business cycle, Marx argued, was an inherent behavioral characteristic of the economy.

The model developed in this chapter focuses on the dynamic operation of the classical economy. It constructs a single-sector macro economy in which the profit cycle is identified as the basic endogenous cycle in Marxist analysis. Other types of crises, including the "disproportionality" crises of a multisectoral model, do not generate cycles that are self-generating and repeating. While randomly caused cycles may serve the purpose of illustrating the instability of the economy, they fail to reveal any long-run time path in the system. The endogenous profit cycle in the Marxist classical economy is of strategic importance because it specifies a time path for business activity that guarantees the regularity of a self-repeating cycle. The model constructed in the following pages focuses on the profit-motivated behavior of capitalists in allocating the economy's total capital stock. Central attention is given to the labor market, and the model is constructed so that the functioning of the capitalist system, as well as its performance over time, is revealed in the dynamic equilibrium path of supply and demand for labor.

II. Marx's Basic Classical Model: Statics

Labor supplied and demanded in the Marxist labor market is necessarily denominated in time units, i.e., hours. The hours of homogeneous labor that are supplied to the market (H^s) are equal to the product of the number of workers employed (N) and the length (in hours) of the working day (h). Accordingly, the supply schedule of labor is expressed as follows:

(1) $H^s = hN.$

It is useful to distinguish two measures of wage that are relevant here. The subsistence wage, first of all, represents an amount of goods that are considered absolutely essential to meet the consumption requirements of the worker and his household.[1] For purposes here we may focus on the *daily* subsistence wage of labor power. In value terms the daily subsistence wage is equal to one day's "necessary labor" (h^*). The second wage measure is the hourly wage (w). The subsistence wage paid daily to the individual laborer may be considered to be the product of the hourly

---

1. Karl Marx, *Capital* (1867), Moscow: Foreign Languages Publishing House, 1961, vol. I, p. 171: "His [the owner of labor power] means of subsistence must . . . be sufficient to maintain him in his normal state as a labouring individual . . . . In a given country, at a given period, the average quantity of the means of subsistence necessary for the labourer is practically known."

wage and the length of the working day,[2] that is,

(2) $h^* = wh$.

The length of the working day is largely the outcome of a bargaining process between the laborers and the capitalists.[3] Bargaining necessarily centers on the length of the working day because workers are motivated only by a given specified subsistence requirement. The individual laborer's supply of labor schedule is unitarily elastic with respect to the real wage. Because of the assumption of a subsistence wage level, higher real wages are not the focus of the bargaining process between capital and labor. When the relative bargaining position of labor is weak, the working day is lengthened; and when labor's relative bargaining position is strong, the length of the working day is shortened. The determinant of labor's relative bargaining position is the unemployment level[4] as specified in the following equation:

---

2. *Ibid.*, p. 548: "From the law: 'the price of labour being given, the daily or weekly wage depends on the quantity of labour expended,' it follows, first of all, that, the lower the price of labour, the greater must be the quantity of labour, or the longer must be the working-day for the labourer to secure even a miserable average-wage. The lowness of the price of labour acts here as a stimulus to the extension of the labour-time. On the other hand, the extension of the working-time produces, in its turn, a fall in the price of labour, and with this a fall in the day's or week's wages. The determination of the price of labour by (daily value of labour power ÷ working day of a given number of hours), shows that a mere prolongation of the working-day lowers the price of labour, if no compensation steps in."

3. *Ibid.*, pp. 234–35: "We see then, that, apart from extremely elastic bounds, the nature of the exchange of commodities itself imposes no limit to the working day, no limit to surplus-labour. The capitalist maintains his rights as a purchaser when he tries to make the working day as long as possible, and to make, whenever possible, two working days out of one. On the other hand, the peculiar nature of the commodity sold implies a limit to its consumption by the purchaser, and the labourer maintains his right as a seller when he wishes to reduce the working day to one of definite normal duration. There is here, therefore, an antimony, right against right, both equally bearing the seal of the law of exchanges. Between equal rights force decides. Hence it is that in the history of capitalist production, the determination of what is a working day, presents itself as the result of a struggle, a struggle between collective capital, i.e., the class of capitalists, and collective labour, i.e., the working class."

4. Cf. the following passages in Marx's *Capital* (vol. I):
   "Taking them as a whole, the general movements of wages are exclusively regulated by the expansion and contraction of the industrial reserve army, and these again correspond to the periodic changes of the industrial cycle. They are, therefore, not determined by the variations of the absolute number of the working population, but by the varying proportions in which the working class is divided into active and reserve army, by the extent to which it is now absorbed, now set free" (p.637).
   "The industrial reserve army, during the periods of stagnation and average prosperity, weighs down the active labour-army; during the periods of over-production and paroxysm, it holds its pretensions in check. Relative surplus population is therefore the pivot upon which the law of demand and supply of labour works. It confines the field of action of this law within the limits absolutely convenient to the activity of exploitation and to the domination of capital" (p. 639).

(3) $h = a + b(1 - N/\bar{N})$,

where $\bar{N}$ is the exogenously given population of workers, N is the number of workers who are employed, and $(\bar{N} - N)$ is the reserve army of unemployed. According to Marx, capitalism is ordinarily characterized by persistent unemployment, that is, $(\bar{N} - N) > 0$. Furthermore, because the capitalist system depends upon the creation of surplus value, it is necessary that $h > h^*$. Since labor's relative bargaining position varies inversely with unemployment, $\Delta h/\Delta(1 - N/\bar{N}) > 0$. That is to say, the working day lengthens when unemployment increases. Substitution of equation (3) into (1) yields a value for the supply of labor:

(4) $H^s = N[a + b(1 - N/\bar{N})]$.

H^s is specified to increase when N increases, thus implying that the percentage change in h resulting from a given change in N is less than the percentage change in N. Stated mathematically, the derivative of H^s with respect to a change in N is positive.

Capitalist demand for labor is a function of the existing total capital stock and the technically determined ratio of constant capital (capital goods plus raw materials) to variable capital (wage goods). The given total capital stock $(\bar{K})$ is divided between constant capital (C) and variable capital (V). By letting $C = rk\beta$ (where k is an index of the quantity of machinery employed, r is the value per unit of machinery, and β is equal to unity plus the ratio of the value of raw materials to the value of machinery employed), $V = wH$ (where wH is the total wage bill), $\sigma = k/H$, and noting from equations (2) and (3) that $w = h^*/[a + b(1 - N/\bar{N})]$, we can express total capital stock as a multiple of H, namely, $\bar{K} = H[r\sigma\beta + h^*/\{a + b(1 - N/\bar{N})\}]$. Rearrangement of these terms gives an equation for the demand for labor:

(5) $H^d = \bar{K}/[r\sigma\beta + h^*/\{a + b(1 - N/\bar{N})\}]$.

Equilibrium in the system exists when

(6) $H^d = H^s$,

or, substituting from above,

(7) $\bar{K}/[r\sigma\beta + h^*/\{a + b(1 - N/\bar{N})\}] = N[a + b(1 - N/\bar{N})]$.

The system is determinate: in addition to the six given parameters $(\bar{N},\bar{K},r,h^*,\sigma,\beta)$, there are five unknowns (w,h,N,H^d,H^s) and five equations ((1)–(3), (5)–(6)). Equation (7) contains those variables to which Marx gave particular attention. There is a unique number of workers employed (N) that equilibrates the system.[5] Specifically, this means an equilibrium unemployment rate, $(1 - N/\overline{N})$.

The wage rate (w) in Marx's analysis is determined simultaneously with the unemployment rate, but it is essentially the unemployment rate that performs the key function of equilibrating the labor market. Associated with each level of unemployment is a unique number of workers employed (N) and a unique extension of the working day (h). From this the total number of hours of labor power delivered to the market is known (that is, $H^s = hN$), and the wage rate is set (since $w = h^*/h$). When the unemployment rate declines the total labor supply is increased, with the number of workers employed growing proportionally more than the work day is shortened. In the same process, both the labor supply and the wage rate increase (i.e., the function relating H^s to w has a positive slope).[6] In terms

---

5. Rearrangement of the terms of equation (7) yields an excess supply of labor function, $EH^s(N)$ that is quadratic in form:

$$EH^s(N) = N^2(-r\sigma\beta b/\overline{N}) + N[h^* + r\sigma\beta(a + b)] - \overline{K}.$$

Because the coefficient of the N^2 is negative, the function relating N and $EH^s(N)$ is a parabola which opens downward. Since, as can be shown, the sign of the discriminant is positive, there are two real roots. (In terms of equation (4), the stipulation that dH/dN is positive over the full range of employment, $0 < N \leq \overline{N}$, means that $a > b$. The discriminant of the quadratic equation, after substitution of $(r\sigma\beta a + h^*)$ for $\overline{K}/\overline{N}$, is $[h^* + r\sigma\beta(a - b)]^2$, and since $a > b$, the sign of the discriminant is clearly positive.) The relevant, or economically meaningful, range of the excess supply function extends from zero to full employment. Were the function to be drawn, with N on the horizontal axis and $EH^s(N)$ on the vertical axis, it would be seen for each specified set of parameter values that zero employment would be associated with a negative excess labor supply with the function intersecting the vertical axis at a point equal to $-\overline{K}/[r\sigma\beta + h^*/(a + b)]$, and that zero excess labor supply would prevail at full employment when $\overline{N} = \overline{K}/[r\sigma\beta + h^*]$. The equilibrium level of employment, N^*, would be the smaller root of the quadratic equation, namely,

$$N^* = [\{h^* + r\sigma\beta(a + b)\} - \sqrt{\{h^* + r\sigma\beta(a + b)\}^2 - 4\overline{K}(r\sigma\beta b/\overline{N})}]/2(r\sigma\beta b/\overline{N}).$$

The equilibrium value of employment may be less than or equal to full employment. Thus the full employment constraint dictates that the smaller root of the function is in the range $0 \leqq N^* \leqq \overline{N}$. Values of the excess labour supply function for levels of employment greater than full employment are of no relevance.

6. The following diagram gives a graphic representation of the functional relationships existing between the labor market variables surveyed in the above paragraph of the text:

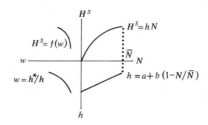

of Marx's analysis, unemployment is an institutional phenomenon—a built-in characteristic of the capitalistic system.

That equilibrium in the Marxist labor market is characterized by unemployment,[7] that is, $(1 - N/\overline{N}) > 0$, contrasts sharply with the full-employment equilibrium solution provided by Marx's contemporary classical economists. Basically, Marx differed from other classical economists in the manner in which the labor supply schedule was specified. (In construction of the labor demand schedule, Marx's model is main-line classical—at least in so far as static analysis is concerned.) The contrast between main-line classical and Marxist labor supply functions is especially sharp in the short-run case. The main-line classical model specified a labor supply schedule that was perfectly inelastic with respect to the wage rate at full employment. Changes in the level of employment were then attributed to shifts in the short-run labor supply schedule brought about by the Malthusian population equation. Marx, by contrast, rejected the Malthusian population equation. Changes in the level of employment meant for Marx changes in the unemployment rate since the size of the total work force (population) was assumed given. Whereas the demand for labor was equated to a full-employment labor supply schedule that was perfectly inelastic with respect to wage in the basic classical model, the demand for labor in the Marxist model was equated with a labor supply schedule that was elastic with respect to wage. Quite simply, then, unemployment was impossible in classical theory prior to Marx's modification of the basic classical model. In its *static* version—in which technological change does not take place and in which we can abstract from capitalists' behavior as concerns decisions to reinvest surplus value— Marxist analysis could conceivably generate a full-employment equilibrium. But such an outcome in the labor market is precluded in Marxist analysis by the *dynamic* behavior of the model. Marx envisaged the capitalists' behavior as concerns decisions to reinvest surplus value— could be only a gross simplification having only heuristic advantages. Analysis of equilibrium conditions of a given unique level of employment was of major concern to classical writers, but represented only an analytical way-station for Marx. This chapter, therefore, now turns to examine the dynamic properties of Marxist analysis. Discussion of the dynamic equilibrium path of the model is found in section IV, V, and VI, following specification of the rate of exploitation and the profit rate in section III.

---

7. Unemployment equilibrium requires that the values of the parameters be such that $a\overline{N} > \overline{K}/[r\sigma\beta + h^*/a]$. Cf. footnote 5.

III. The Profit Rate

The rate of exploitation in Marx's system—perhaps better known as the rate of surplus value—is the ratio of surplus labor to necessary labor.[8] In terms of hours of labor, surplus labor per individual worker is the difference between the length of the working day (h) and the number of hours required ("necessary") to produce the individual laborer's subsistence (h^*).[9] The latter (h^*), referred to in Marx's terminology as necessary labor time, is determined by technical productivity in the wage-goods sector once the historically determined standard of living is given. Substitution from equation (3) yields the rate of exploitation in the following terms:

$$(8) \quad s' = (h - h^*)/h^* = [\{a + b(1 - N/\bar{N})\}/h^*] - 1.$$

Thus, the rate of exploitation is determined directly once the model has been solved for the level of employment, N. When the number of workers employed (N) increases, other things remaining unchanged, unemployment decreases. The resulting increased bargaining strength of labor brings about a shortening of the working day ($\Delta h < 0$) and reduces the rate of exploitation. The rate of exploitation focuses on Marx's claim that the capitalist system depends for its existence upon the exploitation of one social class by another, and—on a more analytical level—provides Marx with a theoretical construct that determines the profit rate and the rate of capital accumulation.

Marx defines the rate of exploitation to be synonymous with the rate of surplus value. The rate of exploitation concept has been used here because it emphasizes the necessary variation in the length of the working day. Creation of surplus value and the exploitation of labor are sides of the same coin. Surplus value can be generated only if the length of the working day (h) exceeds the necessary labor time (h^*). Inasmuch as the length of the working day is a positive function of the unemployment rate, the rate of exploitation varies directly with the unemployment rate. In turn, changes in the rate of exploitation (s') directly affect the profit rate (p') and

---

8. Marx, *op. cit.*, pp. 217ff.

9. *Ibid.*, pp. 216–17: "That portion of the working day, then, during which this reproduction [of the variable capital advanced] takes place, I call '*necessary*' labour-time, and the labour expended during that time I call '*necessary*' labour.... During the second period of the labour-process, that in which his labour is no longer necessary labour, the workman... creates surplus value...."

ultimately affect capitalists' behavior and thereby induce the fluctuations in economic activity that constitute the business cycle.

The rate of exploitation is of key analytical importance in Marx's macro model. Not only does it indicate the *social* origin of capitalists' income, it is a direct determinant of the profit rate. The profit rate (p') is defined as the ratio of surplus value to total capital stock:

(9) $\quad p' = S/\overline{K} = N(h - h^*)/\overline{K} = [(h - h^*)/h^*]/[1 + r\sigma\rho\beta]$
$\quad\quad = [\{a + b(1 - N/\overline{N})\}/h^* - 1]/[1 + r\sigma\rho\beta].$

As equation (9) indicates, the profit rate is resolved into the ratio of the rate of exploitation to the organic composition of capital plus unity. The expression $r\sigma\rho\beta$ is the organic composition of capital, i.e., the ratio of constant capital to variable capital. Here σ is the technically determined ratio of units of machinery to hours of labor, that is, $\sigma = k/H$; r is the price (in labor units) per unit of machinery; $\rho = h/h^*$; and β is equal to unity plus the ratio of the value of raw materials to the value of machinery. The full expression $r\sigma\rho\beta$ thus equals $rk\beta/Nh^*$, the organic composition of capital. Because σ increases over time as technology changes, the profit rate (p') in Marx's classical model declines. With higher values of σ, p' is lower for any given level of unemployment, $(1 - N/\overline{N})$.

IV. Marx's Basic Classical Model: Dynamics

The dynamics underlying Marx's macro model involve continual change in capital stock, technology, and the rate of exploitation. The time paths followed by these variables necessarily describe the economic processes of the classical system—accounting for short-run business cycles as well as the long-run trend. In terms of the Marxist model developed here, dynamic equilibrium may be examined as the condition in which the demand for labor is increasing at the same rate as the supply of labor. As equation (5) implies, the rate of change in labor demanded per period depends not only on the rate of growth of capital stock (which increases the demand for labor), but also on the increase in the ratio of capital goods to labor (σ) and the increase in the rate of exploitation (both of which decrease the demand for labor):

(10) $\quad \dfrac{\dot{H}^d}{H^d} = \dfrac{\dot{K}}{K} - \dfrac{\dot{\sigma}}{\sigma + h^*/\{a + b(1 - N/\overline{N})\}r\beta}$

$$+ \dfrac{b(\dot{N}/\overline{N})h^*}{r\sigma\beta + h^*/\{a + b(1 - N/\overline{N})\}}.$$

Because capital accumulation originates in surplus value, the profit rate may be substituted for the rate of increase in capital stock. Assuming, for the time being, that capitalists invest all surplus value, we have from equations (9) and (10):

$$(11) \quad \frac{\dot{H}^d}{H^d} = \frac{\{a + b(1 - N/\overline{N})\}/h^* - 1}{1 + r\sigma\rho\beta} - \frac{\dot{\sigma}}{\sigma + h^*/\{a + b(1 - N/\overline{N})\}r\beta}$$

$$+ \frac{b(\dot{N}/\overline{N})h^*}{r\sigma\beta + h^*/\{a + b(1 - N/\overline{N})\}}.$$

The supply of labor grows at a rate equal to the rate of increase (decrease) in the number of workers employed plus the rate of decrease (increase) in the length of the working day. The size of the exogenously given labor population ($\overline{N}$) is assumed constant here.

$$(12) \quad \frac{\dot{H}^s}{H^s} = \frac{\dot{N}}{N} - \frac{b(\dot{N}/\overline{N})}{a + b(1 - N/\overline{N})}.$$

Dynamic equilibrium then exists when

$$(13) \quad \frac{\dot{H}^d}{H^d} = \frac{\dot{H}^s}{H^s}.$$

Once equations (11) and (12) are substituted into equation (13), it is seen that we have an equilibrium condition in which there are two unknowns (N and $\dot{\sigma}$) but only one equation. As it stands, therefore, the time path of the model is indeterminate. The one additional equation that is needed may be obtained by specifying technological change to be a function of the unemployment level and the level of technology:

$$(14) \quad \dot{\sigma} = \Psi[(1 - N/\overline{N}), \sigma].$$

The lower the unemployment rate ($1 - N/\overline{N}$), the greater is the inducement for capitalists to substitute capital for labor.[10] Thus $\partial\Psi/\partial(1 - N/\overline{N}) < 0$. The higher the level of the machinery-labor ratio (σ), the greater is the change in the level of σ, that is, $\partial\Psi/\partial\sigma > 0$. The dynamic equilibrium condition is now reduced to one unknown (N) and one equation (equations (11), (12), and (14) substituted into equation (13)):

---

10. Paul M. Sweezy (*The Theory of Capitalist Development* (1942), New York: Monthly Review Press, 1964, p. 88) concludes "That Marx thought of the introduction of labor-saving machinery as a more or less direct response on the part of capitalists to the rising tendency of wages is clearly indicated . . . ."

$$(15) \quad \frac{\dot{N}}{N} - \frac{b(\dot{N}/\overline{N})}{a + b(1 - N/\overline{N})} = \frac{\{a + b(1 - N/\overline{N})\}/h^* - 1}{1 + r\sigma\rho\beta}$$

$$- \frac{\Psi[(1 - N/\overline{N}), \sigma]}{\sigma + h^*/\{a + b(1 - N/\overline{N})\}r\beta}$$

$$+ \frac{b(\dot{N}/\overline{N})h^*}{r\sigma\beta + h^*/\{a + b(1 - N/\overline{N})\}}.$$

V. Marx's Endogenous Business Cycle

The model of Marx's macro system, which has been constructed here, determines dynamic equilibrium at a unique level of employment (unemployment). Such an equilibrium unemployment rate, though feasible, is an unlikely state of dynamic rest for the capitalist economy. The business cycle, a mechanism endemic to the capitalist system, dictates continual oscillations in unemployment with no plateau at either high or low levels of activity. For Marx the business cycle represents the motion of the classical system as it responds to the process of capital accumulation and technological change. The Marxist endogenous cycle has the distinct advantage of demonstrating capitalist instability under those theoretical conditions which other classical economists had believed to assure stability and preclude the theoretical possibility of business fluctuations. *The endogenous cycle does not reject Say's Law:* the surplus value received by the capitalists is completely consumed throughout the course of the endogenous cycle—being either consumed directly by the capitalists or added to the system's capital stock to be consumed in the productive process. In short, Say's Law of Markets is in effect. The endogenous cycle is essentially an unemployment cycle. It is propelled not by breakdowns in the commodity market but by the continuous confrontation between capital and labor in the maelstrom of conflicting pressures emanating from capital accumulation and technological change.

For the sake of expositional simplicity, the condition of dynamic equilibrium developed in section IV of this chapter may be expressed in simplified notational form. Letting $U = (1 - N/\overline{N})$, the unemployment rate, we may express the rate of profit as

$$p'(U, \sigma) = \frac{\{a + b(1 - N/\overline{N})\}/h^* - 1}{1 + r\sigma\rho\beta},$$

where $\partial p'/\partial U > 0$ and $\partial p'/\partial \sigma < 0$; the rate of technological change is

$$\dot{\sigma}(U, \sigma) = \frac{\Psi[(1 - N/\bar{N}), \sigma]}{\sigma + h^*/\{a + b(1 - N/\bar{N})\}r\beta},$$

where $\partial\dot{\sigma}/\partial U < 0$, and $\partial\dot{\sigma}/\partial \sigma > 0$; and the rate of change in the length of the working day, including the remaining terms from equation (15), is

$$\dot{h}(U) = \frac{b(\dot{N}/\bar{N})\{h^*[a + b(1 - N/\bar{N})] - [r\sigma\beta + h^*/(a + b(1 - N/\bar{N}))]\}}{r\sigma\beta[a + b(1 - N/\bar{N})] + h^*},$$

where $\partial\dot{h}/\partial U > 0$, and $\dot{h}(U) = 0$ when $\dot{U} = 0$. In terms of this simplified notation, the dynamic equilibrium condition specified in equation (15) is as follows:

(16) $p'(U, \sigma) - \dot{\sigma}(U, \sigma) = \dot{N}/N + \dot{h}(U).$

As long as the left-hand side of equation (16) is positive, it is clear that the level of employment (unemployment) is increasing (decreasing). Figure 6–1 graphs the function $[p'(U, \sigma) - \dot{\sigma}(U, \sigma)]$ which resembles a form of excess demand function. All points on the function in Figure 6–1 satisfy the condition of dynamic equilibrium but only at unemployment level U_o will the system be at rest in the sense that the unemployment rate will change no further.

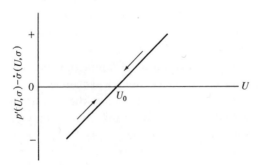

FIGURE 6–1

The main trigger mechanism in the Marxist business cycle is the investment behavior of capitalists.[11] As long as capitalists automatically reinvest all surplus value they receive, the likelihood of a business cycle is considerably reduced, if not eliminated entirely. The system could gravitate to the level of unemployment U_o in Figure 6–1 and remain there indefinitely until the system received some exogenous shock. However, capitalists do not invariably reinvest surplus value. To emphasize this behavioral trait, let α represent the capitalists' propensity to reinvest surplus value. The parameter may be introduced into equation (16) as follows:

$$(17) \quad \alpha[p'(U, \sigma)] - \dot{\sigma}(U, \sigma) = \dot{N}/\overline{N} + \dot{h}(U).$$

We may postulate that there exists some minimum acceptable profit rate $(\bar{p}')$ which the capitalists regard to be inadequate to justify further capital

---

11. In this connection consider the following passages in *Capital*, vol. III (1894):

"...The rate of self-expansion of the total capital, or the rate of profit, being the goad of capitalist production (just as self-expansion of capital is its only purpose), its fall checks the formation of new independent capitals and thus appears as a threat to the development of the capitalist production process. It breeds over-production, speculation, crises and surplus-capital along-side surplus-population" (pp. 236–37).

"...A fall in the rate of profit connected with accumulation necessarily calls forth a competitive struggle. Compensation of a fall in the rate of profit by a rise in the mass of profit applies only to the total social capital and to the big, firmly placed capitalists. The new additional capital operating independently does not enjoy any such compensating conditions. It must still win them, and so it is that a fall in the rate of profit calls forth a competitive struggle among capitalists, not vice versa. To be sure, the competitive struggle is accompanied by a temporary rise in wages and a resultant further temporary fall of the rate of profit. The same occurs when there is an over-production of commodities, when markets are over-stocked" (p. 251).

"...At times too much wealth is produced in its capitalistic, self-contradictory forms. The limitations of the capitalist mode of production comes to the surface:

"(1) In that the development of the productivity of labour creates out of the falling rate of profit a law which at a certain point comes into antagonistic conflict with this development and must be overcome constantly through crises.

"(2) In that the expansion or contraction of production are determined by the appropriation of unpaid labour and the proportion of this unpaid labour to materialized labour in general, or, to speak the language of the capitalists, by profit and the proportion of this profit to the employed capital, thus by a definite rate of profit, rather than the relation of production to social requirements, i.e., to the requirements of socially developed human beings. It is for this reason that the capitalist mode of production meets with barriers at a certain expanded stage of production which, if viewed from the other premise, would reversely have been altogether inadequate. It comes to a standstill at a point fixed by the production and realization of profit, and not the satisfaction of requirements" (p. 253).

accumulation.[12] When this minimum profit rate is reached, capitalists stop net capital accumulation. Capitalists thus respond to the situation $p'(U, \sigma) = \bar{p}'$ by halting further additions to capital stock and directing surplus value to their own consumption. As has been pointed out, the Marxist endogenous cycle exists in the face of Say's Law. For the sake of expositional simplicity, let α be assigned two values, zero and unity. When $p'(U, \sigma) > \bar{p}'$ and $\Delta U < 0$, $\alpha = 1$; and when $p'(U, \sigma) = \bar{p}'$, α switches from unity to zero. When $\alpha = 0$, equation (17) reduces to $-\dot{\sigma}(U, \sigma) = \dot{N}/N + \dot{h}(U, \sigma)$, and indicates that capitalists continue to adopt technological change and increase σ and the organic composition of capital in the process. As net investment is zero, this technological change takes place with a given capital stock. The higher organic composition of capital means a direct replacement of labor by machines. In the process unemployment increases. Until unemployment troughs out at some higher (temporary equilibrium) level, α remains at zero. The economy remains in the trough of the cycle at a high level of unemployment until capitalists perceive that unemployment has stabilized and that the rate of exploitation cannot therefore be expected to rise any further to the advantage of the capitalists. At this point, capitalists decide to resume reinvestment of surplus value. Thus, α switches from zero to unity.

Figure 6–2 illustrates the cycle outlined above. Two dynamic equilibrium paths are drawn: the solid line is drawn for $\alpha = 1$, and the dashed line is for $\alpha = 0$. The horizontal broken line labeled p^* is the difference between $p'(U, \sigma)$ and $\dot{\sigma}(U, \sigma)$ when $p'(U, \sigma) = \bar{p}'$, where $\bar{p}'$ is the minimum acceptable profit rate (see also Figure 6–3). To follow the path of the cycle, let us start at point 1, moving in the boom phase of the cycle with unemployment declining as capital accumulates at a faster rate than the technological displacement of labor. At point 2, the profit rate, $p'(U, \sigma)$,

12. Marx, *op. cit.* (vol. I), p. 620: "The correlation between accumulation of capital and rate of wages is nothing else than the correlation between the unpaid labour transformed into capital, and the additional paid labour necessary for the setting in motion of this additional capital.... If the quantity of unpaid labour supplied by the working-class, and accumulated by the capitalist class, increases so rapidly that its conversion into capital requires an extraordinary addition of paid labour, then wages rise, and, all other circumstances remaining equal, the unpaid labour diminishes in proportion. But *as soon as this diminution touches the point at which the surplus-labour that nourishes capital is no longer supplied in normal quantity, a reaction sets in: a smaller part of revenue is capitalised,* accumulation lags, and the movement or rise in wages receives a check. The rise of wages therefore is confined within limits that not only leave intact the foundations of the capitalistic system, but also secure its reproduction on a progressive scale." Emphasis added.

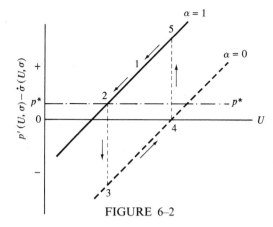

FIGURE 6–2

falls to equality with the minimum acceptable profit rate, $\bar{p}'$, and α switches from unity to zero. The downturn begins immediately. As technological change continues to displace labor and as capitalists refrain from net investment while they replace men with machines, the cycle moves through its recession-depression phase, moving from point 3 to point 4. At point 4, unemployment stops increasing. Capitalists, noting that no further gain can be achieved from further postponement of net capital accumulation, resume investment of surplus value. As a direct consequence, α switches from zero to unity and an instantaneous move from point 4 to point 5 is made. At point 5 the economy is once again in the upswing phase of the cycle. The entire circuit is then rerun.

VI. Further Examination of the Endogenous Cycle

Since both the profit rate function, $p'(U, \sigma)$, and the technological change function, $\dot{\sigma}(U, \sigma)$, depend on the level of the machinery-labor ratio (σ), the two time paths drawn in Figure 6–2 are constantly shifting to the right. As has been stated, $\partial p'/\partial \sigma < 0$ and $\partial \dot{\sigma}/\partial \sigma > 0$. Thus, as the capitalist economy moves from cycle to cycle, the level of unemployment increases from trough to trough (and from peak to peak). The time trend is depicted in Figure 6–3. At some point, the level of unemployment becomes sufficiently high that the system can no longer contain the tensions and class conflicts. At this critical stage (sometimes referred to as the *Zusammenbruch*), the capitalist system breaks down.

When the concept of technological change is broadened to include more

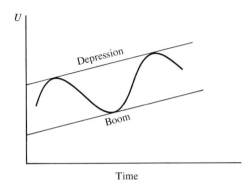

FIGURE 6–3

than the machinery-labor hours ratio (σ), an interesting question arises concerning the possible extinction of the endogenous business cycle. If technological change is specified to affect h^* (necessary labor time), r (price per unit of machinery), and β (unity plus the ratio of the value of raw materials to the value of machinery), the profit function could be written $p' = p'(U, \sigma, h^*, r, \beta)$. Marx made it clear that technological improvement that increases σ may on occasion cause h^*, r, and β to decrease. The impact of technological change thus depends upon the net impact of all four technologically influenced variables. If the changes in h^*, r, and β have a net negative impact, thus causing the function relating p' and U to shift downward and to the right, the analysis of the behavior of the system is unchanged from that presented in this chapter: a self-generating cycle exists. On the other hand, if the net impact of these changes is positive the long-run path of the economic system may be altered. Consider the question in terms of Figure 6–4. The profit function, $p'(U, \sigma)$, the technological change function, $\dot{\sigma}(U, \sigma)$, and the minimum acceptable profit rate ($\bar{p}'$) are drawn in Figure 6–4. If the existing unemployment rate is U_1, the economy is operating in the expansion phase of the cycle, that is, there is a leftward movement along $p'(U, \sigma)$ toward lower levels of unemployment. When $p'(U, \sigma) = \bar{p}'$, expansion halts and the downturn in the cycle begins. In order for this cyclic downturn to be triggered, the minimum acceptable profit level must exceed the profit rate at which an equilibrium unemployment rate exists. As long as $\bar{p}' > [p'(U, \sigma) = \dot{\sigma}(U, \sigma)]$, the system can never establish an equilibrium unemployment rate at a boom level of economic activity. But were a situation to arise such that $\bar{p}' < [p'(U, \sigma) = \dot{\sigma}(U, \sigma)]$, the system would reach an equilibrium unemployment rate

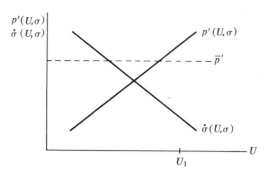

FIGURE 6-4

before hitting any barrier. Were this to happen, the economy would be locked into continuous boom. The profit-linked endogenous business cycle would cease to exist. Now, to consider that the changes in h^*, r, and β have a net positive impact is to specify that the $p'(U, \sigma)$ function in Figure 6-4 shifts upward and to the left over time as technology advances. The $\dot{\sigma}(U, \sigma)$ function, as already indicated, is specified to shift upward to the right as technology advances because introduction of more complex techniques makes it easier to increase the machinery-labor hours ratio still faster. If the $p'(U, \sigma)$ schedule shifts upward to the left over time while the $\dot{\sigma}(U, \sigma)$ schedule also shifts upward to the right, the outcome would clearly be to raise the equilibrium profit rate. Over time the cumulative effect of such changes would inevitably be to create a situation $\bar{p}' < [p'(U, \sigma) = \dot{\sigma}(U, \sigma)]$ in which the profit cycle was entirely eliminated as a self-generating mechanism. Such economic fluctuations as took place would then be in the form of exogenous cycles. The conclusion on this point hinges on the question of the direction in which the $p'(U, \sigma)$ schedule shifts over time. If it shifts upward to the left, the endogenous cycle is eventually eliminated. If the $p'(U, \sigma)$ schedule shifts downward to the right by at least as much as to offset the concurrent shift in the $\dot{\sigma}(U, \sigma)$ schedule, the endogenous cycle will be retained. The formal evidence for the outcome is inconclusive. Nevertheless, Marx's general conviction of the instability of the capitalist system would seem to suggest that the situation Marx envisaged was one in which $\bar{p}' > [p'(U, \sigma) = \dot{\sigma}(U, \sigma)]$, thereby assuring the continued operation of the endogenous profit cycle.

Technological change can also affect the size of the labor force and thereby change the unemployment rate directly. Specifically, techno-logical change may alter the labor participation ratio, $\Omega = \bar{N}/\bar{P}$, where $\bar{P}$

is the given total population. The analysis followed in this presentation has explicitly assumed $\bar{N}$ to be constant. In effect, it has implicitly assumed Ω and $\bar{P}$ to be constant. Yet, as Marx stressed, technological change can alter the composition of the work force and, as women and children are recruited, even change the participation ratio. In terms of the model constructed here (see Figure 6–2), a technologically induced increase in Ω would move the economy into the boom phase of the cycle as capitalists attempted to exploit the profit advantages of the new technology. The increase in Ω would increase unemployment, increase the rate of exploitation, raise the profit rate, and prompt capitalists to accumulate capital until the boom was stopped by a crisis.

Superimposed upon, or short-circuiting the endogenous cycle are a variety of exogenously determined cycles. These exogenously induced cycles can be accommodated by the Marxist macro model constructed here. For instance, abrupt shifts could conceivably occur in the value of α caused by waves of optimism or pessimism that are triggered by environmental variables acting through (psychologically induced) changes in the minimum acceptable profit rate ($\bar{p}'$). Such changes could hasten or delay the downturn of the cycle. A further source of exogenous disturbance might exist in the flow of technological change which may come in fits and starts as innovations bunch together from time to time.

VII. The Source of Instability in Marx's Two-Sector Model

As has been seen in Chapter 5, Malthus's two-sector model, which defines sectors according to type of labor employed, shows the precariousness of equilibrium in a system dependent on a unique pattern of expenditures. In a similar vein, Marx's two-sector model, which, however, defines sectors according to type of commodity produced, gives even greater emphasis to the precarious nature of market equilibrium. The interdependency theme in Marx's two-sector model is accentuated by the underlying presumption that commodities are use-specific and capital is non-adaptable between categories. This is in sharp contrast to the single-sector model in which production is of "goods in general." The single-sector model does not define a fixed dividing line between commodity categories of fixed and variable capital and it permits commodities to be shifted between categories at will. The use-specific character of output in the two-sector model dictates that the composition of output and the composition of capitalists' expenditures be delicately balanced so that the economy's total output in each commodity group is demanded and no unwanted commodity inventory accumulates. If the parameters of the system are not perfectly synchronized with the expenditure pattern of the capitalists, the output of the system is "disproportional."

The two sectors of Marx's two-sector model both engage in commodity production. Accordingly, both sectors employ productive labor. The first sector (Department 1) produces the means of production, i.e., machines and raw materials; the second sector (Department 2) produces wage goods, i.e., foodstuffs, means of subsistence for labor. The functional division between these two sectors is set precisely along lines dictated by Marx's definition of capital, according to which the total capital stock is sub-divided into constant capital (machines plus raw materials) and variable capital (wage goods). Commodity production in each Department is a function of the quantity of capital employed in that Department. Part of each Department's output is absorbed by internal demand for replacement of capital stock consumed in production; the remainder is placed on the inter-Departmental market. It is the task of the two-sector model to demonstrate that equilibrium involves a delicate balancing of reciprocal relationships in the system. Specifically, technologically determined production coefficients must have a precise set of values such as to assure that the two Departments, together with the capitalists as a class, purchase the total marketed output. According to Marx, there is no smoothly function-ing mechanism that automatically assures equilibrium.

The relationships can be formulated in the following way. In each Department, gross output (Q_i^*) is a function of the capital stock (K_i) allocated to that Department. Assuming that the wage rate is given, the relationship may be stated simply in linear form:

(1) $Q_i^* = x_i K_i$.

Since a portion of each Department's output is demanded internally in order to replenish the Department-produced part of total capital stock, only the remaining portion is placed on the inter-Deparmental market. That is,

(2) $Q_i^s = Q_i^*(1 - y_i) = x_i K_i(1 - y_i)$,

where Q_i^s is the physical quantity of the ith commodity supplied to the market, and y_i is the fraction of gross output set aside by the producing

Department. As more total capital stock is employed in a given Department, that Department's demand increases for the output of the other Department. This inter-Departmental demand is expressly linked to the composition of capital in each Department, and by definition, the more total capital employed in a Department, the greater is the employment of both constant and variable capital. Thus, inter-Departmental demand for replenishment of capital stock is specified as $Q_i^d = c_j K_j$, where $i = 1, 2$; $j = 1, 2$; and $i \neq j$. The marketed supply of commodity "surplus" that is then set up for sale is

$$(3) \quad q_i^s = \overline{K}[\xi x_i (1 - y_i) - c_j (1 - \xi)],$$

where ξ is the proportion of total capital stock employed in Department 1; $1 - \xi$ is the proportion employed in Department 2; and $\overline{K}$ is the given total capital stock with the prices per unit of constant capital and of variable capital assumed given. These physical quantities on the left side of equation (3) constitute the profit share of total output. That is to say, the profit of the system measured in physical units amounts to the quantities of Q_1 and Q_2 produced in excess of capital replacement (depreciation) requirements.[13] The existence of profit, an inseparable characteristic of the capitalistic system, means that the parameters of equation (3) for a two-Department model must have values such that $c_2/x_1(1 - y_1) \leqq \xi/(1 - \xi)$ $> c_1/x_2(1 - y_2)$, where numerical subscripts designate Department. In the case of static equilibrium—Marx's case of simple reproduction—the total capital stock is allocated between the two Departments so that $\xi/(1 - \xi) = c_2/x_1(1 - y_1)$. In this case $q_1^s = 0$ and all of q_2^s is consumed by the capitalists. By contrast, economic growth requires[14] positive amounts of both q_1 and q_2. This means a distribution of total capital stock such that $c_2/$

---

13. *Ibid.,* p. 580: "The annual production must in the first place furnish all those objects (use-values) from which the material components of capital, used up in the course of the year, have to be replaced. Deducting these there remains the net or surplus-product, in which the surplus-value lies."

14. *Ibid.,* pp. 580–81: "To accumulate it is necessary to convert a portion of the surplus product into capital. But we cannot, except by a miracle, convert into capital anything but such articles as can be employed in the labour-process (i.e., means of production), and such further articles as are suitable for the sustenance of the labourer (i.e., means of subsistence). Consequently, a part of the annual surplus-labour must have been applied to the production of additional means of production and subsistence, over and above the quantity of these things required to replace the capital advanced. In one word, surplus-value is convertible into capital solely because the surplus-product whose value it is, already comprises the material elements of new capital."

$x_1(1 - y_1) < \xi/(1 - \xi) > c_1/x_2(1 - y_2)$. In this latter case, it is possible for total capital stock, comprised of constant and variable capital, to be increased.

Demand for the net product or surplus of the system is generated entirely by the capitalists, who either consume or invest their profit income.[15] The demand for constant capital or q_1 goods, originates entirely from investment demand:

(4a) $q_1^d = I.$

The demand for q_2 goods, on the other hand, is derived from both the demand for variable capital as well as the luxury and subsistence consumption of the capitalist class:

(4b) $q_2^d = eI + C.$

Here, e is a parameter that denotes the ratio at which q_2 and q_1 goods are added to total capital stock. It is a weighted average q_2/q_1 ratio determined by both (a) the projected technological relation of labor to constant capital and (b) the expected average wage rate,[16] with the relative weight of the two factors set by the proportion of net investment allocated respectively to Departments 1 and 2. As long as the profit rate exceeds the minimum acceptable profit rate, investment demand expands until a resource constraint, either of q_1 or q_2, is encountered. The consumption expenditure of the capitalists is set on an ad hoc basis. With the demand side of the model thus specified, equilibrium may or may not prevail. The outcome is indeterminate:

(5a) $q_1^d \leq q_1^s$, and

(5b) $q_2^d \leq q_2^s.$

Excess supply is as likely an outcome as equilibrium, and in this way the precariousness of the outcome is stressed by Marx.

---

15. *Ibid.,* p. 591: "One portion [of profit] is consumed by the capitalists as revenue [i.e., private consumption], the other is employed as capital, [and] is accumulated."

16. Because capital accumulation reduces the unemployment rate and causes the wage rate to rise, the amount allocated to wage goods must exceed the wage bill for the planned net addition to the work force by an amount equal to the change in the wage bill for all previously employed labor. In other words, if m is the expected hourly wage in q_2 units, the total investment outlay for wage goods is equal to $(m\Delta H + H\Delta m)$, of which $m\Delta H$ is paid to the net addition in the work force, Δm is the expected rise in the hourly wage, and $H\Delta m$ is the increased expenditure for the prior existing work force.

Given the distribution of total capital stock between the two Departments, the quantities of q_1 and q_2 are determined. Equilibrium in the system requires that the capitalists' expenditures fully absorb the entire profit or surplus value. To do this, the capitalists either consume or invest. While consumption is limited to q_2 goods, investment requires both q_1 and q_2 goods combined in specific proportions. Balanced growth, perhaps the simplest case to consider, requires that the capital stock increase in the same proportion in each Department. If investment demand plus consumption demand do not absorb exactly all commodity surpluses, the system is out of equilibrium. "Disproportionality" then exists and crisis may ensure.

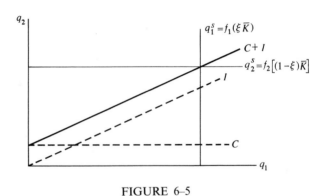

FIGURE 6–5

In Figure 6–5 the commodity surpluses for Departments 1 and 2 are drawn. Here, for a given total stock of capital $q_1^s = Q_1^s - Q_1^d = f_1(\xi \overline{K})$, and $q_2^s = Q_2^s - Q_2^d = f_2([1 - \xi]\overline{K})$, where $f_1' > 0$ and $f_2' > 0$. Since ξ, the proportion of total capital stock employed in Department 1, is assumed given, the quantities of q_1 and q_2 are known and are drawn as straight line functions. The ratio of q_1 to q_2 that is required for balanced expansion of the capital stock in the two Departments is represented by I, the investment expansion path. Capitalist consumption of q_2 goods is drawn as schedule C. Combined together, the $I + C$ schedule must intersect at the same point at which the q_1 and q_2 schedules intersect, i.e., at the upper right-hand corner of Figure 6–5, if equilibrium is to prevail. Any significant part of either commodity supply that is not employed by the capitalist will occasion an adjustment crisis. Undesired inventories of q_1 and/or q_2

mean a reduction in realized surplus value and a fall in the profit rate.[17] If the magnitude of excess supply is sufficiently large, the drop in the profit rate will trigger the downturn of the business cycle. In terms of Figure 6–4, a disproportionality crisis causes a sharp downward (to the right) shift in the $p'(U, \sigma)$ schedule. If, at the existing level of unemployment, the realized profit rate is then pushed below the minimum acceptable profit rate, the system is shoved into the recession phase of the cycle. Once triggered by this exogenous disturbance, the course of the business cycle is that described by Figure 6–2 and the accompanying discussion in the text.

---

17. Marx, *op. cit.* (vol. III), pp. 620–21: "If the use-value of individual commodities depends on whether they satisfy a particular need then the use-value of the mass of the social product depends on whether it satisfies the quantitatively definite social need for each particular kind of product in an adequate manner, and whether the labour is therefore proportionately distributed among the different spheres in keeping with these social needs, which are quantitatively circumscribed.... The social need, that is, the use-value on a social scale, appears here as a determining factor for the amount of total social labour-time which is expended in various specific spheres or production.... For instance, let us assume that proportionally too much cotton goods have been produced, although only the labour-time necessary under the prevailing conditions is incorporated in this total cloth production. But in general too much social labor has been expended in this particular line; in other words, a portion of this product is useless. It is therefore sold solely as if it had been produced in the necessary proportion. This quantitative limit to the quota of social labour-time available for the various particular spheres of production is but a more developed expression of the law of value in general, although the necessary labour-time assumes a different meaning here. Only just so much of it is required for the satisfaction of social needs. The limitation occurring here is due to the use-value. Society can use only so much of its total labour-time for this particular kind of product under prevailing conditions of production."

To recast Marx's conceptualization of the problem, we may conceive of the average profit rate as the ratio of realized surplus value to capital stock, that is, $\sum(S_i - Z_i)/\sum K_i$, where S_i is surplus value, Z_i is the value of unwanted inventory, K_i is capital stock, and the subscript denotes Department. Clearly, the appearance of unsold inventories reduces the average profit rate.

Epilogue 7
The Close of the Classical System

beginning with the Quesnaysian Revolution and the emergence of classical theory, the structure of economic analysis was dominated for well over a century by the classical concept of capital. In the last three decades of the nineteenth century, a sea change in economic analysis took place. As a consequence of the momentous contributions in the early 1870's, most importantly by Léon Walras, the classical system of analysis was closed.[1] The structure or general schema of economic theory was revamped and the classical approach was displaced as the conceptual framework for economic inquiry. Central to this structural shift in economic theory is the redefinition of the capital concept. The developments in economic theory in the 1870's pushed capital from the leading role it had played in economic analysis. Since the classical capital concept had formed the structural framework of the classical system, its displacement meant the demise of classical theory itself. It is interesting to note the unabrupt way in which the structural shift took place: the close of the classical system resembles more closely an ideational synthesis than a scientific revolution. There was something of an inner dialectic present in the analytical developments of the 1870's inasmuch as the same theoretical contributions that formed the capstone in the edifice of classical theory

---

1. Carl Menger, *Principles of Economics* (1871), Glencoe, Illinois: The Free Press, 1950. W. Stanley Jevons, *The Theory of Political Economy*, London: Macmillan, 1871; 2nd edition, 1879. Léon Walras, *Elements of Pure Economics* (1874–77), Homewood, Illinois: Richard D. Irwin, 1954.

served as the cornerstone for the post-classical economics. The direct critiques of classical theory had no significant impact on the structural shift. For the most part, redefinition of capital was accomplished as a serendipitous consequence of inquiries initially designed to draw together loose ends of the classical system. The developments that caused the demise of classical economics were not the victorious elements of a frontal clash on a paradigmatic frontier. Classical economics fell largely because the citadel was overturned from within. It is the purpose of this chapter to discuss the main forces that contributed to the close of the classical system. Details of the structure of post-classical theory will not be dealt with here.

I. The Redefinition of Capital

As has been detailed in preceding chapters, classical theory defined capital to consist of prior accumulated commodity stocks which constituted the all-inclusive input into the production process. Classical capital consists of three main commodity groups: wage goods, raw materials, and machines. The commodity composition of these groupings is not rigidly drawn. Quantities of specific commodities are differently allocated between the main groupings depending on technology and on supply-demand conditions in the labor market. The dominant classical tradition bracketed together the first two commodity groups (wage goods and raw materials) as "circulating capital" and referred to the third group (machines) as "fixed capital." K. Marx rearranged these three commodity groups: wage goods, taken by themselves, were labeled "variable capital" while raw materials were combined with machines under the rubric of "constant capital." The two approaches are but slight variations on the dominant classical theme that commodities are produced by means of commodities. Both versions emphasize that all inputs into the productive process are employed either directly in their commodity form (raw materials and machines) or are employed in their transformed mode of labor power, being first transformed into labor by means of exchange in the labor market. All commodities in the classical system's total capital stock are specified to be on hand at the outset of the production period. Capital, in other words, consists of those productive commodities which are set aside at the end of one year for employment in production the following year. Nowhere is this point more clearly seen than in the instance of wage goods. In terms of classical theory, wage goods are necessarily previously accumulated stocks. Workers are paid out of past production, or more specifically, out of past accumulations from past production. Moreover, workers are paid this year not because they are contributing to current output per se, but rather because labor has a relative scarcity value given the state of technology and the magnitude of the economy's total capital stock. The wage bill, and hence the quantity of wage goods, is determined concurrently with the wage rate (cf. Chapter 3). As classical economists explained it, wages could be paid because capitalists had abstained from consumption. The savings of the capitalists, not the productivity of labor power, was the origin of the wage bill. Given all this as a direct outgrowth of the classical capital concept, it is perhaps not surprising that K. Marx chose the labor theory of value as the argument to assert labor's claim over current production.

The "new economics" of the 1870's completely deleted the wage-goods component from the accepted definition of capital. For the Austrian school led by Carl Menger, wage goods comprised the category of commodities that is *not* included in capital stock. According to the Austrian definition, wage goods are *goods of first order*—that is to say, commodities of final consumption which provide direct utility to the consumer. Capital comprises all other commodities. Referred to as *goods of higher order*, the commodities that make up capital are intermediate products—raw materials, goods in process, active inventories, and machines—which are used in their commodity form as inputs in the productive process. The character of capital goods is to be understood in terms of the time structure of production. In the Austrian model, production of final consumption goods is conceptualized as taking place in several sequential stages: the output of each successive stage of production becomes the commodity input in the following stage. Since all productive activity is directed to the task of creating final consumption goods (products that directly provide utility to consumers), the commodities that make up the capital stock are ever becoming, ever undergoing metamorphosis. The commodities that comprise the capital stock are combined with labor (and land) at each stage of production and are ultimately worked up into consumption goods. These goods are "intermediate" in the sense that they are located in the sequence of production between the elemental factors of production (labor and land) and commodities of final utility.[2] They are the means of production, not the ultimate end of production.

The conceptualization of capital formulated by Léon Walras represents the sharpest break with the classical tradition (see Table 7–1). The Walrasian definition greatly reduced the commodity composition of the capital concept. From the classical definition, only the machinery component was retained. Both wage goods and raw materials were excluded as commodity components of capital stock. Capital, in Walras's view, is fixed capital, namely "all durable goods... which are not used up at all or are used up only after a lapse of time."[3] Productive capital—specifically, what Walras designates as *capital proper*—generates productive services.[4] It comprises such commodities as machines, instruments, tools, office buildings, factories, workshops, and warehouses.[5] Those commodities which comprise wage goods and raw materials (two categories of goods which were included as integral components of the classical definition of capital) were defined by Walras to constitute income.[6] The

---

2. It is important to emphasize that capital takes the physical form of machines, raw materials, goods in process, etc. Attempts to calculate the value of the total capital stock have proceeded on the assumption that the major proportion of value added in each stage of production is derived from labor; "waiting" or roundaboutness accounts for the remainder of value added. On this premise, economists have reduced or transformed capital stock into wage-goods units and have reckoned the value of the total capital stock as the total accumulated expenditure of wage goods for labor employed in the past to fabricate currently existing intermediate goods. Unfortunately, the procedure of expressing capital stock as a fund of value calculated in wage-goods units has been confused to mean that capital stock *is* a wages fund. The unit measuring capital is thus mistaken for the substance of capital itself. It should suffice to repeat that capital consists of intermediate goods (goods of higher order). Although capital is fabricated by means of the elemental factors of production, labor and land, and can be interpreted (since wage goods are paid to the owners of labor services and land services) to be the transformed embodiment of wage goods, the fact remains that capital is a category of goods that has its own distinctly separate identity. As E. Böhm-Bawerk (*Positive Theory of Capital* (1899), South Holland, Illinois: Libertarian Press, 1959, p. 73) points out in this connection: "The concept of capital as an aggregate of intermediate products... is the choice which I consider the better. If that is the decision, then the workers' means of subsistence will not fall within the concept of capital."

3. Walras, *op. cit.,* p. 212.

4. *Ibid.,* p. 218.

5. Consumers' durables, which include such commodities as dwelling-houses, public buildings, furniture, and art objects, are also termed capital goods proper by Walras, but since this set of goods produces consumers' services rather than productive services they are recognized to comprise a separate category of goods. Because we are concerned here with comparing the classical and post-classical approach to the production process, we can abstract from consumers' durables.

6. Walras, *op. cit.,* p. 212.

distinction between capital and income hinges on the difference between a stock and a flow. Capital (a stock) is measured at a point of time while income (a flow) is measured over time. Capital is a stock on hand at the outset of production while income is the flow of output that is forthcoming during the production period. Walras also distinguishes between capital and income by means of the simple criterion of whether a commodity can be used more than once or only once. For Walras, income goods are used but once while producer goods are used several times. The former is durable, the latter is consumed entirely upon the first use. The definition served Walras's purposes admirably well.

TABLE 7–1

Definitions of Capital

Commodity Group	Capital Concepts			
	Classical		Post-Classical	
	Quesnay/ Smith	Marx	Austrian	Walrasian
Wage Goods	Circulat- ing Capital	Variable Capital		
Raw Materials		Constant Capital	Capital ("inter- mediate goods")	
Durable Producers' Goods (machines, tools, etc.)	Fixed Capital			Capital Proper

Above all, the Walrasian concept of capital greatly diminished the importance of the capital concept. Capital, which had served as the unifying construct in the classical economics, became a term designating but one of several productive inputs. In the Walrasian system, capital is on equal footing with labor and land. As is revealed in Table 7–1, the inclusiveness of the capital concept was trimmed and narrowed substantially. The change was part of a broader restructuring of economic analysis; it was a manifestation of a structural change in economic theory. The displacement of the classical capital concept signaled the demise of classical economic theory, though in this case symptom and cause are closely intertwined.

II. Simultaneity in Economic Analysis: Capstone and Cornerstone

The period-analytic approach of classical economic theory subdivided or compartmentalized economic analysis in a way that singled out production and exchange for separate treatment. The factor market and the product market were treated as largely independent of one another. They were defined to attain equilibrium in sequential steps. That is to say, the total capital stock is allocated and the labor market equilibrated at the outset of the production period. Then, once the goods are produced, the total commodity output (less allowances for internal consumption in each industry) is bought and sold on the product market during the exchange period. When capital stock is reconstituted, the scene is then set for the next production period. Capital accumulation is thus prior to production, and production is prior to the marketing of commodities. The approach itself emanates from the classical capital concept. The bifurcation of classical analysis into time-separated product and factor markets is also revealed in the time-lagged relationship between labor's product and labor's wage. The latter is the basis for J. S. Mill's dictum that "demand for commodities is not demand for labor." According to classical theory, workers are paid from past periods' output; labor's real earnings (i.e., the wage goods purchased with the wage bill) are not produced in the current period. In the basic classical model the wage rate (and hence the wage bill) is determined by the relative scarcity of labor and is not immediately linked to the productive contribution of labor.[7]

Theoretical developments of the 1870's were steps toward specifying the relationships of classical analysis in terms of a simultaneous model. The step was most crucial since the overturning of the period-analytic approach spelled the collapse of the main structure of classical analysis.

---

7. F. W. Taussig, writing in the mid-1890's, clearly recognized the importance of simultaneity in economic analysis for the definition of capital: "In the active controversy on the wages-fund doctrine which has been going on during the last quarter of a century, the question has gradually come more and more into the foreground whether wages come from the current product of labor or from a past product" (*Wages and Capital* (1896), New York: Augustus M. Kelley, 1968, p. 1).

Both the Austrian and the Walrasian approaches stressed that the factor markets and the product markets were highly interdependent. More importantly, this interdependence is viewed to be simultaneous. The Austrian model stresses that product prices are of decisive importance for the determination of factor prices. Specifically, factor prices are imputed back from the market prices established for finished products. The line of causation implied is unidirectional: the prices of higher order goods being a function of the prices of first order goods. The wage bill in the Austrian model contrasts most sharply with the basic classical model. For the Austrian theory, the real wages paid in the current period are generated by current production. The wage goods marketed and consumed are those produced during the current period. Labor inputs and wage-goods output belong to the same time period. What classical theory treated as a stock the Austrian approach treated as a flow. Wage goods thus constitute a component of income, not of capital stock. The distinction was to become a hallmark of the new economics.

Simultaneous interdependence between factor and product markets is even more strongly emphasized in Walrasian theory which became the basis for the post-classical paradigm. Walras's synthesis of classical theory is complete: it metamorphosed the classical system and formulated a new conceptual framework for economic theory that has dominated the field of theoretical inquiry in the twentieth century. Capital is defined narrowly by Walras to comprise machines (tools, factories, etc.). The production process à la Walras involves no transformation of wage goods into labor power as part of the metamorphosis of capital. Walras's productive "capital proper" is joined directly with other elemental factors of production, namely, labor and land, in the fabrication of goods and services. Walrasian general equilibrium, in its essential aspects, joins together the factor market and product market in a system in which equilibrium in both markets is simultaneously established. Time lags, such as existed in classical analysis, are eliminated. Factor market and product market are joined together by the relationships between two main groups of decision makers who participate in each market. These groups are (1) entrepreneurs and (2) individuals who comprise the general public. The entrepreneurs act as buyers in the factor market and as sellers in the product market. At the same time members of the general public act as sellers in the factor market and as buyers in the product market. The costs of production, namely, the expenditures made by the entrepreneurs to obtain the services of labor, land, and capital in the production process, are identical to the incomes (wages, rent, interest) received by suppliers of these factors of production. In the product market, the total expenditures of the general public, which are derived from the incomes received, are identical to the sales revenue of the entrepreneurs.

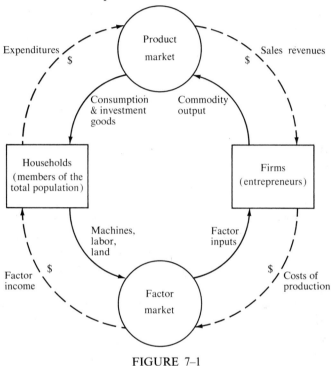

FIGURE 7–1

The outline of the system is described in Figure 7–1. Given the dominance of Walrasian analysis over twentieth-century economics, it is not surprising that this flow diagram is a familiar expository device. So ingrained is it in the contemporary approach to economics that, in one variation or another, it is used in most every introductory course in economics. It is difficult for the contemporary economist to think of a time when the mind of the economist could find novelty in the simultaneous circular flow. Nevertheless, a brief review at this point is not out of place. In Figure 7–1 the members of the general public, located in the box on the left, make all decisions concerning supply of the factors of production and demand for the economy's commodity output. The entrepreneurs, located in the box on the right, make all decisions concerning the direction of production activity in response to the preferences of the sovereign consumer. That is to say, they make all decisions relating to the demand for factor inputs and the supply of commodity outputs. Capital (machines), labor (the laboring population), and land are stocks of factors owned and/or controlled by members of the general public. The flow of services of all three categories is bought and sold in the factor market. Ultimate payment for these services takes the form of the economy's output of goods. In this context, the classical categories of wage goods and raw materials appear only as flow variables. The means of subsistence for the population as well as the raw material requirements for production are consumed in the same period in which they are produced. The simultaneous system was constructed by Walras in a way that compelled analysis of concurrent interdependencies among variables. Classical concepts, which served admirably well in an approach that stressed sequential step-wise analysis, had to be displaced. The major change, of course, was the necessary redefinition of the classical capital concept. As a consequence of such changes, theoretical inquiry could no longer operate in the normal way within the confines of the classical structure.

In retrospect we can say that Walras's general equilibrium model put together some significant loose ends of classical theory. By explicating the neglected relationship between factor and product markets, Walras's system was a natural extension of classical inquiry. But, clearly, it was more than just another building block in the construction of the classical system. It formed, in effect, the capstone of the classical conceptual structure. In this context Walras may be termed the last great classical economist. But his accomplishment is much more pivotal in the history of economic thought. Janus-like, the Walrasian system is situated between two great systems of economic theory. It forms the capstone to classical theory on the one side, and on the other the cornerstone to the modern post-classical theory. It provided answers to questions posed by the normal progression of theoretical inquiry within the classical framework. But at the same time it posed new questions that were to occupy the attention and time of economists during the following century.

III. Decision Units and Decision Criteria

The centrality of capital in classical economic theory placed the capitalist in the role of the dominant decision-maker in the classical system. At the outset of the production period, capitalists set commodities and labor into motion. It was their function to allocate the total capital stock and direct the production of the economy's commodity output. As profit maximizers, classical capitalists adjusted the inter-industry allocation of capital so as to equalize the profit rate everywhere in the economy. In the process of establishing a uniform profit rate, capitalists brought about adjustments in the composition of commodity output and in the relative quantities of industry output supplied to the market. Classical theory did not elaborate a theory of the "firm" to explain the maximization behavior of capitalists. Neither did classical economics provide a theory of laborers as decision makers who volitionally determined the short-run labor supply. Although classical theory's population equation set the decision criteria for the long-run labor supply, it was not until the 1870's that an explanation of short-run labor supply is set in terms of decision criteria followed by individual members of the work force. Similarly, the decision component inherent in commodity purchases is not touched upon by classical theory. In all, the classical system is quite elitist in concept. Capitalists lead; all other groups in society follow. Laborers and landlords, though naturally indispensable for economic activity, are assigned negligible roles as decision makers. Analysis is conducted in terms of aggregate or class units. Although allusion is not infrequently made to individuals (generally for purposes of illustration), classical economic theory had no place for the common man. Capitalists controlled the significant decision variables of the model, and the primary emphasis of analysis was placed on matters relating to the control, allocation, and accumulation of capital.

The shift that took place in economic theory during the generation following the appearance of Walras's *Elements of Pure Economics* (1874–77) brought about a complete recasting of the *dramatis personae* of economic analysis. The capitalist class, which served classical theory so well as a hypothetical construct, was removed completely from the center of the stage. In effect, the concept of the capitalist class was subdivided into two parts: (1) ownership and (2) control. The term capitalist is reserved by Walras to designate an individual who owns capital stock. As thusly defined, capitalists are placed on equal footing with laborers and landowners. Accordingly, the elite character of the capitalist class is eliminated from the mainstream of economic analysis. The term "entrepreneur" is popularized to designate the control function previously assigned to the capitalists. The entrepreneur is a hypothetical construct whose assigned function in the Walrasian system is to direct and co-ordinate production activity. In the factor market, entrepreneurs partici-pate as buyers of factor inputs; and in the product market they take the role of suppliers of commodities. Profit maximizing, with the producing unit or firm serving as the unit of organization, is the objective of their decisions, just as it was the goal of classical capitalists. Functionally, there is little difference between the Walrasian entrepreneur and the classical capitalist as decision agents in control of production. The setting in which each is located, however, differs markedly because of the different time structure of the theoretical models in which the two function: the Walras-ian entrepreneur operates in a simultaneous system with the current hire of factors linked explicitly to current demand for commodities, whereas the classical capitalist operates in a time-lagged system with the current hire of factors tied to the net accumulations of capital from past periods. After the 1870's, when the rise of marginal productivity analysis opened up the theoretical possibility for factor substitution to take place, the post-classical entrepreneur was assigned the additional task to select the technology (i.e., production function) as a further dimension to profit maximization.[8]

Conceptualizing the "general public" as decision makers is a very great departure in the analysis of economic behavior. In its egalitarian over-tones, this intellectual development of the 1870's intriguingly parallels the late nineteenth-century trend in Western Europe toward universal (male) suffrage. The general public in Walras's general equilibrium model participates in the factor market as suppliers of factor services and enters the product market as demanders of commodities. Members of the general public function as utility maximizers. Each individual adjusts the composi-tion of his or her commodity purchases so as to obtain the greatest possible consumer utility from a given budget. Formally, the individual accom-plishes this by equating the marginal utility per dollar spent on each and every commodity included in his or her market basket. In making labor supply decisions, each laborer moves to equate the marginal disutility of work with the marginal utility of income. Individual laborers thus operate

8. The simultaneity of the Walrasian or post-classical model pointed directly to the set of relationships made explicit in marginal productivity analysis. Because the model emphasizes that current factor hire is tied directly to current product demand, it was just a short step to argue that each factor is paid due to its productive contribution. Working out marginal productivity theory followed from the simultaneous justaposition of factor and product markets—a simple, yet fundamental change in economic analysis.

in both markets to maximize their personal utility. The marginal utility approach was an indispensable adjunct to the simultaneous analysis of Walrasian general equilibrium. By specifically setting down decision criteria or behavior guidelines for members of the general public, it permitted a calculus in which the vast majority of the general population would participate in voicing their preferences and voting their income in the market place. It provided the basis for analysis of demand decisions in the commodity market as well as the basis for study of supply decisions in the factor market. In a sense, the marginal utility approach democratized economic theory and made every person influential, to some degree, in the outcome of economic activity. Not only did this have the effect of opening up a whole new area for study (a whole new set of puzzles for practitioners to solve and with which they have been occupied for the past century), it also contributed greatly to shifting economic inquiry away from a hypothetical world dominated by the capitalists of classical theory. Attention shifted increasingly to price which became the central construct of post-classical theory. The behavior of participants in the economic process was viewed in terms of its relationship to price; and price data were considered to form a major input into the decision process of entrepreneurs and members of the general public.

IV. Conclusion

Developments in economic theory during the period that spans more than a century between the Quesnaysian Revolution (1759) and the Walrasian Synthesis (1874) are most readily interpreted and comprehended in terms of the centrality of the capital concept first propounded by F. Quesnay. The classical capital concept provided the essential unity to economic theorizing during this period and posed questions that set the direction of theoretical inquiry. In the process, the structure of theories which emerged further emphasized the key role of the classical capital concept. This study of classical economic theory is a retrospective, historical view of the pattern and structure of the significant economic theories that "fit" together and display inherent unity in their dependence upon the classical capital concept. Capital, specifically the classical concept, is thus the hallmark of classical economic theory. When developments in economic theory in the 1870's caused the eventual abandonment of the classical capital concept, the lodestar of classical theory was plucked from out of the heavens. The structure of classical theory collapsed; a major reorientation of theoretical inquiry took place; and a new economics began to take shape. The demise of classical economics was not abrupt, however. It took a generation before the old professors died off—and even then classical theory fell more to disuse than to disrepute. Classical approaches to many problems continued to appear. J. S. Mill's *Principles* continued to serve as a standard text in both Britain and the United States. The shift in economic theory did not mean that all parts of classical analysis were forgotten or set aside. Quite the contrary: parts of the "old" were slowly incorporated and blended with the "new." (A. Marshall probably represents this adaptation process best.) Though the old ideas faded slowly, nothing new was being cut from out of the classical quarry (with one obvious exception of K. Wicksell's independent rediscovery of H. Thornton's theory of currency creation). The significant new contributions being made after 1870 were rooted in the post-classical approaches to economic analysis. In them we can clearly discern the forces of change that closed the classical system.

Index